"My fascination with film sound began wnen I was just a kid, and I would have *loved* to have had this book back then! It's a brilliant overview of what we do as sound designers, and I hope it will inspire the creativity in everyone who reads it."
—STEVE LEE, sound effects wrangler (*Lion King, Apollo 13, A Goofy Movie*), founder of The Hollywood Sound Museum

"Ric is the premier sound effects guru! We use tons of his stuff in our creative works. He has encouraged us all to Make Some Noise!"
—LESLIE BRATHWAITE, multi–Grammy-winning mix engineer, Pharrell Williams, Michael Jackson, Outkast

"It's undeniable that Ric is the king of the sound effects world."
—KLAYTON (CELLDWELLER), artist/musician/synthesist, *Transformers—The Last Knight*; *Deadpool*; *Teenage Mutant Ninja Turtles: Out Of The Shadows*

"Ric Viers has written an easy-to-read and well thought-out book for teens. I wish this fantastic resource was available when I was in junior high and high school. Covering everything from affordable gear, DIY recording techniques, and other tips, his book is Absolutely Valuable! This is a must read!"
—WATSON WU, composer/sound designer, Assassin's Creed video game, Transformers video game, Need for Speed video game

"A definitive how-to tome in the process and thinking behind recording, designing, and using sound effects in modern media. It offers up a terrific breadth of techniques and mindsets to do amazing sound work. Ric has mapped out all the necessities in understanding microphones and recording techniques that any enthusiast of sound will find useful in maximizing their creative efforts. A definite must read, and a great addition to the best literature in the field."
—CHARLES MAYNES, sound designer/sound effects recordist/re-recording mixer, *Spiderman; Jumanji: Welcome to the Jungle; Fantastic Four*

M★KE

SOUND EFFECTS RECORDING

SOME

FOR TEENS

NOISE

RIC VIERS

MICHAEL WIESE PRODUCTIONS

Published by Michael Wiese Productions
12400 Ventura Blvd. #1111
Studio City, CA 91604
(818) 379-8799, (818) 986-3408 (FAX)
mw@mwp.com
www.mwp.com

Cover design by Johnny Ink. www.johnnyink.com
Copyediting by David Wright
Printed by McNaughton & Gunn

Manufactured in the United States of America

Library of Congress Cataloging-in-Publication Data

Names: Viers, Ric, author.
Title: Make some noise : sound effects recording for teens / by Ric Viers.
Description: Studio City, CA : Michael Wiese Productions, [2018]
Identifiers: LCCN 2017029438 | ISBN 9781615932726
Subjects: LCSH: Sound--Recording and reproducing--Amateurs' manuals.
Classification: LCC TK7881.4 .V5394 2018 | DDC 621.389/3--dc23
LC record available at https://lccn.loc.gov/2017029438

Printed on Recycled Stock

ACKNOWLEDGEMENTS

Thanks to everyone who helped
make this book possible!

Sean Viers for being an awesome son and
agreeing to help with the book.

Erik Steele for shooting the cool photos.

Chris "Boris" Trevino for proofreading the
manuscript, helping with the screenshots
and being an awesome friend.

And all the Detroit Chop Shop interns,
past, present and future...

Thanks for helping me make some noise!

TABLE OF CONTENTS

FOREWORD

Welcome friends to the Make Some Noise family...
My earliest memories of recording sound were back
in the late '70s. I used this really funky "portable" analog
tape machine that took cassette tapes. I would set it up in
my basement underneath the wooden stairs and wait for
someone to walk down and I would press the two buttons
and then listen back to the wooden creaks and imagine
scary movie scenes. In my generation, there were not
many field recorders available or any digital audio workstations to listen back with. I never thought that thirty years
later I would have a career of recording sounds for a living.

Today, it is much easier to pick up a recorder and start
capturing sounds. But without the correct advice from a
professional you will be prone to bad recording habits
that will just equal up to bad sounds!

Make Some Noise by Ric Viers is the perfect solution
and a great guide that not only helps you understand
the fundamentals of sound effects recording but also is
a great companion that steers you in the correct direction so your recordings will be as good as those of any
professional out there. *Make Some Noise* will also give
you the knowledge of what to do once recordings are
created, how to name files properly, and the concept
of metadata.

I met Ric Viers in 2006 in Hollywood while recording sounds for a film called *Poseidon*. Ric and I hit it off immediately talking about recording and sharing great stories for hours! I learned right away that Ric is a wealth of information for anything sound related and most importantly how to have fun doing it!

Make Some Noise is no exception! Recording sound effects is an extremely fun process and this book will keep the fun factor in the mix as well as share some of Hollywood's greatest recording secrets. You will never treat a stalk of celery the same!

Without further ado, welcome to the world of Ric Viers' *Make Some Noise*.

—**Charlie Campagna**, sound effects recordist, designer, Hollywood, CA — *Iron Man 3*; *The Hunger Games*; *Mad Max: Fury Road*; *Skyfall*

PREFACE

Anyone can make sound effects. All you need is a recorder and a microphone to get started. Honest.

When I first got started recording sound effects, I knew nothing about the business. Nothing. At the time, I was working as a freelancer recording dialogue for movies and television shows. I knew how to use microphones and recorders, but I knew nothing about making sound effects. In less than a year of making sound effects in a spare bedroom of my apartment, I created sounds that would eventually be used in *Halo*, *Sons Of Anarchy* and even *LEGO Batman*. So, if I can do it, you can do it too.

The good news is that the information inside this book will guide you through all the tricks and techniques I wish I knew when I was back at my apartment getting started. I've also included tips on how to use the gear and tons of ideas for recording projects, including one hundred sound effects you can make at home. There are also lots of pictures and diagrams to help it all make sense and my son Sean Viers has agreed to add his comments at the end of each chapter to give his perspective on the topics.

Just remember, sound effects recording is like photography, except instead of a camera, you are using a microphone. Everyone can take pictures, so anyone can record sound effects.

Now let's make some noise!

Ric Viers

 AN INTRODUCTION TO SOUND EFFECTS

■ WHAT ARE SOUND EFFECTS?

A sound effect is any recorded or performed sound used to represent action or activity. This could be as simple as the sound of birds chirping in a subdivision or as complicated as a spaceship landing in your backyard. Some people like to record sound effects as a hobby, but most people record sound effects for one of two reasons. The first reason is they are working on a project that needs a specific sound effect. The second reason is they want to make sound effects to sell online. Whatever your reason is for creating sound effects, we'll go over each step in the process to help you get started making noise.

Sound effects are heard everywhere, everyday. They are used in big blockbuster movies like *Transformers*, television shows like *The Flash*, and video games like *Call Of Duty*. Sound effects help make the story come to life by immersing viewers and players in the sonic world of what they're experiencing. However, all of these sounds are created and added to the production at the end of the process during what is called post-production (literally meaning "after the production").

Iron Man **painting courtesy of Detroit artist Thomas Savage**

So, the footsteps you heard Iron Man make in *The Avengers* were actually recorded and added long after Robert Downey Jr. took off the iconic suit. And the sound of the missiles he shoots was probably just a combination of fireworks and jet plane flybys layered together. Audiences expect to hear the sounds of things they see on the screen so it is up to the filmmakers to provide those sounds. In fact, people are so used to hearing sound that modern day digital devices have sound effects added to them to recreate the sounds made by their mechanical predecessors like telephones, doorbells and even washing machines! Welcome to the magical world of sound effects.

Let's discuss the five main types of sound effects:

1. Hard Effects
2. Foley Sound Effects
3. Background Effects
4. Production Elements
5. Sound Design Effects

HARD EFFECTS

Hard effects are sounds that represent a literal action in a movie, video game or app. These are the most commonly recognized sound effects. Sounds in this category include things like doorbells, dog barks, and punches. Once recorded, these literal sounds can be reused for many different things in the future.

FOLEY SOUND EFFECTS

Foley is the art of performing sound effects while watching a movie or a video clip. Typical sounds found in this category include footsteps, prop handling like picking items up and setting them down, cloth movements like fabrics moving along with the actor and other interactions between characters like shaking hands and hugging each other. Foley sound effects help bring the characters and their actions to life.

Note: Although these types of sounds are generally recorded while watching a video, you can record these types of sounds anywhere without watching a screen.

BACKGROUND EFFECTS

Background sound effects are ambient sounds in a scene and are sometimes referred to as ambiences or atmos. These types of sounds help tell the audience where the scene is taking place and possibly what time of day it is. For example, the sound of birds chirping tells the audience that it is morning time, whereas the sound of crickets chirping tells the audience that it is nighttime. Background sound effects can also provide a consistent bed of sound for a scene that was shot with multiple takes that have inconsistent background sounds.

PRODUCTION ELEMENTS

Production elements are sounds that are typically used for graphics, scene transitions and other title effects. There are many types of production elements, but the main ones that are used are hits, whooshes and stingers. These sounds bring otherwise silent graphics to life and are commonly heard in movie trailers.

SOUND DESIGN EFFECTS

Sound design effects are sounds that are too difficult to record in real life or the sounds of things that don't actually exist. For example, your project might include a dinosaur roaring, but unfortunately, dinosaurs aren't around anymore to record. Or, you might need the sound of the interior of the International Space Station. Sure, it exists and it is possible to record this, but getting the clearance from NASA or having the budget to arrange the recording expedition is probably not an option. To create these sounds you'll need to recreate the sound using whatever resources you have. This means you'll need to record material to work with and manipulate the sound in a DAW (Digital Audio Workstation). But don't worry; we'll get to all that good stuff later on.

■ WHY SOUND EFFECTS ARE IMPORTANT

Sound effects are the missing ingredient in many productions. Whether it's a big-time Hollywood movie, the latest top-shelf video game or your next YouTube vid, sound effects play a large role in making the action come to life. While there are tons of sound effects that have been produced over the years, the best sound effects are the ones that are uniquely created for a project. This book will show you how to record, edit and create your own sound effects without leaving your house!

Sound is really important. George Lucas, the director of *Star Wars*, once said that sound is fifty percent of the moviegoing experience. Some filmmakers argue that sound is even more important. Try this experiment: Watch an action scene from your favorite movie, especially one with gunshots, explosions, fist fights and car chases, but watch the scene without the sound.

Just watch. Now, play the scene again, but this time close your eyes and just listen to the scene. Which time did you notice the biggest impact on your senses? Undoubtedly, you chose the one with sound. Why? Because, sound is really important.

Lucas's *Star Wars* is probably the most notable film that raised the bar for sound effects in movies. Sound guru Ben Burtt was responsible for creating the sounds of the spaceships, droids, lightsabers, blasters and all of the other sounds from far, far away. Up until the late 1970s, it was common practice to use synthesizers and theremins for science fiction sounds or simply reuse sounds that had already been created and used in other films. Burtt had a much different approach. He wanted to create all new material for the film. So, he grabbed his recorder and started recording and experimenting with different sounds to see what he liked. The results of his experiments have changed the sound of cinema forever. It was Burtt's passion to try new things and to think outside of the box that was the key to creating the out-of-this-world sounds in the film.

When *Star Wars* was released, filmmakers and sound designers began to take the sounds in movies more seriously. It didn't take long for the video game industry to catch up either. You can now play most video games in 5.1 surround sound with some titles offering DTS soundtracks. This is drastically different than the old mono sound during the beginning days of Atari systems. Audiences of all forms of media are now accustomed to well-prepared sound effects. They notice when sound is missing or is poorly produced. So, it's up to you to give them great sound!

— SEAN'S NOTES —

Sound is very important and I notice it in movies and TV all of the time. I love to play video games and the surround sound really adds a lot to the game play. Just remember that sound effects are important and they make an action have a feel to it because of the sound accompanying it.

CHAPTER 2

RECORDING GEAR

Recording sound effects is a lot of fun, but in order to record sound effects you need to learn how all of the gear works first. Let's start off with the basics about how sound works and then we'll discuss the gear used to record sound.

■ WHAT IS SOUND?

Since this book is all about recording sound, it's important to understand what sound is and how it works. The human ear perceives vibrations in air molecules as sound. These vibrations produce sound waves similar to the ripples in a pond that are created when you drop a rock into water. The ripples spread out from the source of the splash and head in every direction until they lose energy. Sound works the same way, but travels in every direction including up and down, whereas the ripples in a pond spread out horizontally.

SOUND WAVES

A sound wave is created when something vibrates and sends enough energy out to cause the surrounding air molecules to vibrate. When air molecules vibrate, they compact tightly together (called a "compression") and then pull apart (called a "rarefaction"). Every time air is compressed from one direction, it tries to pull apart in the opposite direction, which causes another compression. This spreads the energy outwards. One compression and the rarefaction that follows is called a wave cycle. The distance traveled over one wave cycle is known as the wavelength.

Note: Sound waves can be created in mediums other than air molecules, such as metals, wood and even water. For the purpose of this book, we will focus on the vibrations of air molecules.

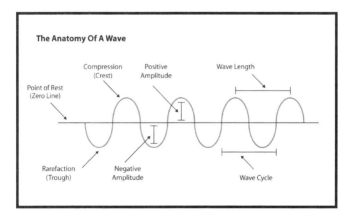

The Anatomy Of A Wave

FREQUENCY

Frequency is the number of wave cycles that occur per second. We perceive frequency as the pitch of a sound. Higher frequencies are perceived as higher pitches and lower frequencies are perceived as lower pitches. Sound moves at a constant speed through air. This means that as the frequency of a sound increases, its wavelength gets shorter. Higher frequency sounds have more wave cycles occur in one second than lower frequencies.

Frequency is measured in Hertz (abbreviated as Hz). The human ear can detect frequencies between 20Hz and 20kHz. The "k" in 20kHz stands for "kilo," which is taken from the Metric system, and means one thousand. So, 20kHz is the same as 20,000Hz. Sounds that occur below 20Hz (known as "infrasonic") and above 20,000Hz (known as "ultrasonic") are out of our range of hearing. We, as humans, do not perceive these frequencies as sound. However, some animals like cats and dogs can hear well above the 20kHz range. In fact, dogs can hear up to 40kHz (twice the range of humans), cats can hear up to nearly 80kHz, and dolphins can hear up to 150kHz.

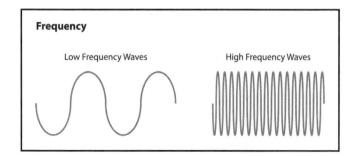

Frequency

Low Frequency Waves

High Frequency Waves

The audible frequency range is often simplified into three main categories: lows, mids, and highs. In simple terms, the low range is often referred to as "bass," the mid range is referred to as "mids," and the high range is referred to as "treble."

MAIN FREQUENCY RANGES

Low Range or Bass: 20Hz–200Hz
Mid Range or Mids: 200Hz–5KHz
High Range or Treble: 5KHz–20KHz

AMPLITUDE

Amplitude is the amount of energy present in a wave cycle, and is measured in decibels (abbreviated as "dB"). Our ears interpret amplitude as volume. We interpret sound waves with a lot of amplitude as being loud, or high in volume. Conversely, we interpret sound waves with only a small amount of amplitude as being quiet, or low in volume.

The shape of our inner ear affects the way we perceive volume as well. Our ears are more sensitive to hearing mid-range frequencies, especially in the 1kHz to 4kHz range, than lower frequencies. This means that even if two frequencies have the same amplitude, we do not necessarily perceive them as being the same volume as each other. You can test this yourself by finding a tone generator online or in a DAW or app and sweeping through the frequencies while keeping your amplitude same level.

When you raise the volume of a sound by 6dB, we perceive this as being twice the volume. When you lower the volume of a sound by -6db, the human ear perceives this as being half the volume.

Going back to our metaphor of sound being like dropping a rock into a pond can help you understand amplitude better. If you drop a large and heavy rock into the pond, it will produce large waves. We would perceive these large waves as a loud sound. If we drop a tiny pebble into the pond, though, it produces tiny waves. We would perceive this as a quiet sound. In the same way that you can see the waves in the pond, you will also see the waves of your sound when you look at your recordings in a DAW.

Screenshot of waveform in the digital audio workstation Reaper

■ WHAT YOU NEED TO GET STARTED

While all of the technical descriptions and definitions are important to know when recording, the good news is that producing cool sound effects is more creative than it is technical. So if you've got a good imagination, you've got a head start! Don't worry too much about all the numbers and science behind sound. That stuff will make sense after you've been recording for a while. Now, let's talk about what equipment you'll need to get started.

To record sound effects all you need to get started is a microphone, a recorder, and a pair of headphones. The microphone allows you to collect the sound. The recorder allows you to store the sound for later use. And the headphones allow you to listen to what you are recording. Sound recording equipment can be pretty complicated and very expensive. However, technology has advanced to the point where you can visit most electronic retail stores in your area and find the gear you need for a few hundred dollars. To put this in perspective, my first recording package cost over $10,000. Today, there are standalone handheld recorders that come with a built-in stereo microphone that can be purchased for less than $200! Let's take a closer look at how each component of the recording package works.

Handheld Recorder

In this book, we will assume you are using a handheld recorder to record your sound effects. This will allow us to focus on the fun part—making noise! If you are looking for more advanced recording techniques, check out my book The Sound Effects Bible.

■ THE MICROPHONE

A microphone works by sensing vibrations in air molecules in the same way that the human ear does, except a microphone uses a diaphragm instead of the eardrum and has electronics inside it that convert acoustic sound into an electrical signal. Headphones work the same way, but in the opposite direction by converting an electrical signal into acoustic sound.

Microphones typically come in mono or stereo. A mono microphone is the most common and it contains one capsule to capture sound. A stereo microphone uses two capsules to capture a stereo image by pointing one capsule to the left and the other capsule to the right. The microphone on the top of most handheld recorders is a stereo microphone and therefore has two capsules.

POLAR PATTERNS

Microphones capture sound in different directions. The directionality of a microphone is known as its polar pattern. When a sound occurs within the polar pattern of a microphone, it will sound the most natural and is considered to be on-axis or on-mic. When a sound occurs outside the polar pattern of a microphone, it will sound weak or thin and is considered to be off-axis or off-microphone. It's important to know what type of polar pattern (sometimes called a "pickup pattern") your microphone has so that you know how to position your microphone when capturing a sound.

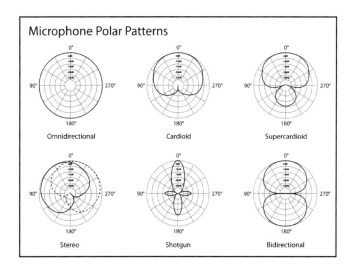

Here's an overview of some of the main polar patterns used in recording sound effects:

- Omnidirectional Pattern
- Cardioid Pattern
- Hypercardioid Pattern
- Supercardioid Pattern
- Stereo Polar Pattern

OMNIDIRECTIONAL POLAR PATTERN

Omnidirectional means "to receive equally from all directions." A microphone with an omnidirectional polar pattern (often shortened to omni) captures sound in every direction.

CARDIOID POLAR PATTERN

The cardioid polar pattern gets its name from its heart-shaped pickup pattern. This pattern captures directly in front of the microphone as well as some from the sides. It has a null in its rear, which means that doesn't pick up any sound from behind.

HYPERCARDIOID POLAR PATTERN

A hypercardioid pattern is similar to a cardioid pattern. It captures sound in a narrower shape in front of the microphone than a cardioid, which helps prevent it from picking up sounds coming from the sides of the microphone. Unlike cardioid microphones, hypercardioid microphones will pick up some sound from behind.

SUPERCARDIOID POLAR PATTERN

A supercardioid is a very narrow polar pattern. It captures sound mainly from a small area in front of it, as well as slightly from a small area on its sides and rear.

These microphones are called "shotgun microphones." The shotgun microphone is probably the most commonly used microphone for recording dialogue in movies because it mainly captures what is directly in front of the capsule. This is very useful for recording clean sounds that are free of background noise.

STEREO POLAR PATTERN

Stereo microphones are very useful for capturing the sense of space in an environment or the sound of an object moving within that environment. Typically, each capsule in a stereo microphone has a cardioid polar pattern. When the two polar patterns overlap they create a sense of direction in the sound.

CHOOSING A POLAR PATTERN

Shotgun microphones and stereo microphones are the most commonly used microphones for sound effects recording. If you'd like to get an external microphone to record sound effects, you should start with a shotgun microphone, since you can use your handheld recorder as a stereo microphone. This will give you more options when you record. If you can afford the upgrade, you'll find that you can get better sound. If you can't afford the upgrade, don't worry. The built-in microphones are a great start.

WIND NOISE

Microphones can capture the tiniest vibrations in the air. Because they are so sensitive, they are extremely vulnerable to wind movement. Even the slightest breeze in the air can cause an undesirable low rumble or distortion in your recording. You may not notice wind as much if you use inexpensive headphones to record or listen back to your recordings on smaller speakers. Even if you can't hear it, you'll learn to see wind noise in your DAW once you get more experienced. To reduce and sometimes completely eliminate wind movement from reaching the diaphragm of the microphone, you'll need to use one of the following wind protectors:

1. Windscreen
2. Windshield
3. Blimp/Zeppelin

WINDSCREENS

Windscreens are custom-made pieces of foam that fit your microphone to protect the capsule from excessive air movement. Windscreens are useful when working indoors, but are not very effective outdoors. Be sure not to touch the windscreen while recording because the microphone will capture the rubbing sound.

Windscreen

WINDSHIELD

Windshields (commonly called blimps or zeppelins) are the ultimate form of wind and vibration protection. A blimp comprises three basic parts. The first part is the internal shock mount, which helps isolate your microphone from vibrations. Then, there is a hollow tube with a thin fabric membrane that encapsulates the shock mount and your microphone. This tube creates a pocket of still air around your mic. In order for outside wind to get to your microphone, it needs to both travel through the tube's fabric (where it loses energy) and then move the still air around your microphone (where it loses even more energy). The final layer of wind protection comes from the windshield that wraps around the hollow tube of the blimp. Most blimps have a handheld grip, also known as a pistol grip, that you can comfortably hold or mount onto either a boom pole or microphone stand. Blimps can be used indoors, but their wind-blocking benefits are best heard when used outdoors with a windshield on top.

Windshield

FUR WINDSHIELDS

Fur windshields offer much better protection from wind and air movement than foam windscreens. Fake fur is used instead of foam which helps isolate the microphone from a windy environment. It is very rare to see a professional sound recordist use a microphone outside without using a fur windshield over their microphone.

Fur Windshield covering a Blimp

Fur windshields come in all shapes and sizes and have different names given to them by the companies that make them. Rode Microphones, a major microphone manufacturer, has unique names for their different fur windshields, like Dead Cat, Dead Kitten, Dead Wombat, etc. Rumor has it that the names got their origins from the fact that the windshields tend to look like road kill.

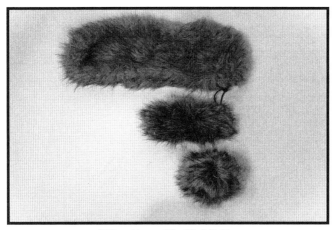

Different types of Fur Windshields

Most handheld recorders come with a custom wind-screen to fit the built-in microphone on the recorder. These are very helpful for reducing wind noise, but if you want the ultimate protection for your microphone, it's a good idea to upgrade to a fur windshield like the WS-11 Windscreen from TASCAM, which fits most popular brands of handheld recorders. Wind protection is a must-have for recording outdoors.

■ HANDLING NOISE

Most microphones are very sensitive, so if you shake them or handle them too much the microphone will make a rumbling sound. This is called "handling noise." Here are a few tools to use to help you reduce handling noise:

1. Shock Mounts
2. Microphone Stands
3. Boom Poles

SHOCK MOUNTS

To reduce handling noise you can use a shock mount, which uses rubber bands to help isolate the microphone from vibrations. Some shock mounts can be used with handheld recorders and if you can afford one, it will make it easier to get better sound.

Shock Mount

MICROPHONE STANDS

Microphone stands do a lot of the hard work for you. When you hold a microphone or handheld recorder, you risk the chance of your arm getting tired. This results in a shaky hand that can cause handling noise in the recording or even worse—your arm gets too tired to point the microphone in the right place. Using a microphone stand will take care of both problems by keeping the microphone pointed in the same place throughout the recording without wearing out your arm. This is especially useful when you're recording long takes of ambiences.

Note: Mounting a handheld recorder on a microphone stand may require a special mic thread adapter. You can find these adapters online at places like www.guitarcenter.com or www.bhphotovideo.com.

Microphone Stand Adapter

While microphone stands are a huge help, they can also be a bit troublesome because you have to carry them around wherever you go. In the end, using a microphone stand is a big plus if you don't mind lugging around the extra baggage. Five minutes doesn't seem like a long time until you're holding a microphone steady. Then, five minutes seems like an hour.

Microphone stands that have a boom arm are the best to use for sound effects recording because they give better positioning options for the microphone. A useful tip to keep the boom arm from sagging is to point the long end of the arm in the same direction that you tighten the lever to lock the boom arm into place. When the force of gravity pulls your microphone down it will tighten the lever more so that the microphone won't sag or fall. Be sure to use a microphone stand that has a tripod base with three legs for extra stability. When using the boom arm, position the boom arm parallel to one of the legs to prevent the stand from falling over.

Mic Stand with Boom Arm

BOOM POLES

Boom poles (sometimes called fish poles) are extendable microphone stands that you hold with your hands. Because they are handheld, care should be taken to avoid handling noise. The benefit of using a boom pole is that it can get your microphone closer to the action. Boom poles come in different lengths and some of them extend as far as twenty feet! The boom pole is one of the main tools for recording dialogue in movies.

Using a Boom Pole to Record the Smoke Stack of a Steam Engine

Boom poles are useful for recording things like birds high up in a tree, following someone on a skateboard, or staying above someone swimming in a pool. You can use a shock mount to mount your microphone or handheld recorder to the end of the pole. Boom poles are typically used with external microphones. If you're using a handheld recorder on the end of a boom pole, you won't be able to reach the controls on the recorder to make adjustments and you'll also need a headphone extension cable to reach the end of the pole. Some recorders come with a remote control that will allow you to make changes remotely.

EXTERNAL MICROPHONES

Most handheld recorders include XLR jacks on the unit to allow you to plug an external microphone into it. There are hundreds of microphone models to choose from and they can be used to pick up sound differently. The only catch is that sometimes the microphones can cost more than the handheld recorder.

Every microphone has advantages and disadvantages. Some are made with better quality; some have unique polar patterns, some record in mono, some record in stereo, and some record in surround sound with six channels of audio. Here's a brief overview of some of the types of microphones that you can experiment with:

SHOTGUN

Shotgun microphones are highly directional and designed to reduce a significant amount of sound coming from the sides of the microphone. This design makes these microphones the best choice for recording dialogue outdoors as well as sound effects.

Shotgun Microphone

STEREO MICROPHONE

Stereo microphones have two small diaphragm capsules to allow the microphone to capture two mono signals to create a stereo image in the sound. The placement of the capsules is typically in a fixed XY pattern, although some microphones allow you to adjust the width of the stereo image. If you have the ability to make this adjustment, experiment with different settings to see which sound you like best. When in doubt, leave the microphone in the XY position.

Stereo Microphone

LARGE DIAPHRAGM

Large diaphragm microphones are typically found in studios and are often used to record vocals for songs and Foley sound effects. These microphones have a diaphragm (also called a capsule) of 1″ or greater.

Large Diaphragm Microphone

SMALL DIAPHRAGM

Small diaphragm microphones have a capsule of 1″ or less (typically around ½″) and are found in studios and sometimes in live music recording sessions.

Small Diaphragm Microphone

BINAURAL MICROPHONE

A binaural microphone looks like a human head and is used to simulate the way humans hear sound by using two microphones positioned on opposite sides of the head. The recorded sounds are specifically intended for listening through headphones, as the recordings do not typically translate well over speakers.

Binaural Microphone

HYDROPHONE

A hydrophone is a waterproofed microphone used for recording sound in water. While there are a few tricks for recording underwater with regular microphones, it's best to use hydrophones for underwater work.

Hydrophone

CONTACT MICROPHONE

Technically called a piezoelectric microphone and some-times a pickup microphone, contact microphones are unique in that they record sound traveling through solid objects and not through the air. Unlike other microphones, you need to mount a contact microphone to an object with tape or putty in order to record. These are fun microphones to experiment with.

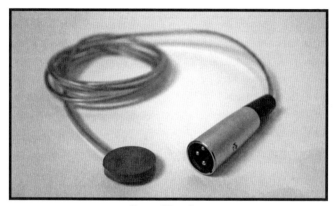

Contact Microphone

PICKUP COIL MICROPHONE

Also sometimes referred to as coil pickups, a pickup coil microphone is another specialty microphone like the contact microphone. Pickup coil microphones are used to record the usually unheard electronic signals from things like phones or computer hard drives. Most pickup coils have a suction cup built in to allow you to mount them to flat surfaces. These are also cool microphones to experiment with, as they reveal a whole world of sound that we normally can't hear.

PZM

PZM microphones (pressure zone microphone) are specifically designed for placement near a boundary such as a table surface or wall to capture a wider range of sound in the area. For this reason, they are also called boundary microphones, and are often used on the boards of a hockey rink to pick up the sounds of the players during the game or at the front of a stage to capture actors talking in theater performances.

PZM

LAVALIER

Lavalier microphones, also known as lavs, are really tiny microphones designed for miking actors, interviews, or on-air talent. For sound effects recording, lavs can be useful for taping onto objects to get a very up-close sound.

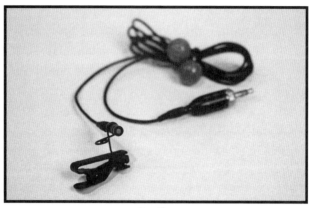

Lavalier

■ THE RECORDER

The recorder is the heart of your recording package. All audio will flow in and out of this device. The microphone's signal will go into the recorder through the recorder's input. The signal is recorded on a storage medium inside of the recorder. The sound is monitored through the headphone's output. Essentially, the recorder is your portable studio.

DIGITAL STORAGE

Today, all modern recorders are digital. This means that the recordings are converted into a digital format on the recorder and stored internally or on a removable memory card, typically an SD card. In the days of analog tape, recordings were kept on the tape that you originally recorded on for archiving purposes. Any time you wanted to use a recording, you'd copy it off your original tape. Tapes weren't re-used that much for recording because the audio quality of analog tape gets worse as you re-use it. However, digital storage, be it internal storage on your recorder or external memory cards, is not affected by re-use, and can be used over and over again without affecting your recordings' audio quality. This means that if you want to re-use your memory cards, you need to keep track of what data has been transferred and archived. Failing to do this could result in not having enough storage to work with during your next recording session or even worse, accidentally erasing sounds that you worked hard to record because you forgot to transfer the data. Get in the habit of transferring your data at the end of each session before you put the gear away.

RECORDER SETTINGS

Every recorder is different and has different buttons and menus to use. Some offer a few selections to make, while others offer a wealth of options to change and tweak. When you get a new recorder, take a few minutes to get familiar with all of the menus and what all the buttons do. Be sure to refer to the manual for anything you don't understand.

Here's a list of common buttons and menu selections found on most recorders and some tips on how to use them:

1. Int./Ext. Mic
2. Mic/Line Level

3. Phantom Power
4. Low Cut/High Pass
5. Record, Stop, Pause
6. File Type
7. Sample Rate/Bit Depth
8. Microphone Recording Level/Input Level
9. Headphone Level
10. Mono/Stereo
11. Internal Speaker

INT./EXT. MIC (INTERNAL/EXTERNAL MICROPHONE)

This option allows you to select the built-in microphone (Int. Mic) or the XLR inputs on the recorder for using an external microphone (Ext. Mic).

MIC/LINE LEVEL

This option allows you to choose which audio level is selected for recorders with XLR inputs. XLR jacks are the professional standard connectors for microphones. Some hybrid jacks will have both XLR and TRS (often called ¼″). This allows you to use XLR for microphones (Mic Level) or TRS for audio devices (Line Level).

XLR/TRS Combination Jacks on the TASCAM DR-40 Handheld Recorder

PHANTOM POWER

Some microphones require a separate power source called "phantom power" to allow the microphone to work. If you are using an external microphone, check the microphone's manual to see if the microphone requires phantom power. If it does, you'll need to turn on phantom power via the recorder's menu or an external switch on the recorder. Otherwise, your microphone will not work properly. Note that some microphones have an internal battery compartment to power the microphone with phantom power. If you decide to use an internal battery, be sure that the battery is fresh and check to see if there is an additional switch on the microphone to turn phantom power on. External phantom power supplies can be purchased if your microphone or recorder doesn't have a way of supplying phantom power.

LOW CUT/HIGH PASS

Low cut (also called "high pass") allows the recorder to reduce the amount of low frequencies that are recorded. This function goes by both names because it cuts out low frequencies and lets the higher frequencies pass through unaffected. While a windscreen will greatly reduce low rumble from sources like wind movement, sometimes you may still need to use a low cut to eliminate the rumble. Low cuts are also useful when nearby low frequencies can be heard from things like large trucks, air conditioning hum, etc. In general, try to avoid using a low cut unless it's necessary because a lack of low frequencies can make your recording sound thin.

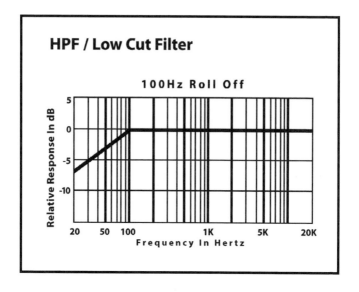

RECORD, STOP, PAUSE

The record, stop and pause buttons seem self-explanatory; however, some recorders have different functions assigned to them. For example, on some recorders pressing "record" places the recorder in a recording standby mode where you can see your levels and hear what's coming into your microphones but doesn't actually record until you hit the record button again. Some recorders also use the pause button to start a new take. Refer to the recorder's manual and experiment with these buttons so that you are familiar with how the buttons function on your unit.

The first rule of recording is make sure that you are recording! Some recorders have either a red light or a counter with numbers that increase while recording. Always verify you are recording. You'd be surprised how many times even the professionals forget to press record.

FILE TYPE

Recorders usually allow you to choose between the industry standard .wav file (pronounced "wave") and the consumer standard .mp3 file. MP3 files are compressed and much smaller so they use as little as 5% of the storage space that .wav files do. However, .wav files are uncompressed and will make your recordings sound better as well as allow you to edit and process the sound later without losing the quality of the recording. It's better to record in the .wav file format even if you plan on using the sounds as .mp3 files later. Remember, you can always convert your quality .wav files to .mp3s when you're finished editing them. If you have the option to choose, always choose to record in .wav format.

SAMPLE RATE/BIT DEPTH

Every second, a digital recorder takes a certain number of snapshots of the sound that it is picking up, converts it into digital data, and stitches it together into what we perceive as one continuous sound. The amount of snapshots, or samples, that a recorder takes per second is known as its "sample rate."

Professional CD audio is sampled at 44.1kHz, which means the recorder takes 44,100 snapshots per second. While that may seem like a lot, professional audio is often recorded at sample rates as high as 96,000 times and even 192,000 times per second. The higher the sample rate, the more information is recorded. This can be very useful when editing and processing the sounds later, especially if you plan on doing a lot of pitch shifting and processing to the sound. The only catch is that higher sample rates use more storage space. Since 96kHz is more than twice the amount of samples as 44.1kHz, it uses more than twice the amount of storage space. You need to record at a minimum sample rate of 44.1kHz to capture the full audible spectrum of sound for humans.

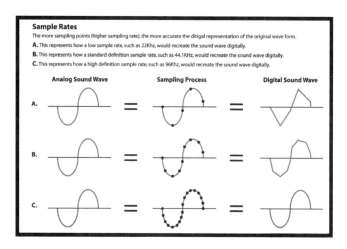

Sample Rates
The more sampling points (higher sampling rate), the more accurate the ditigal representation of the original wave form.
A. This represents how a low sample rate, such as 22Khz, would recreate the sound wave digitally.
B. This represents how a standard definition sample rate, such as 44.1KHz, would recreate the sound wave digitally.
C. This represents how a high definition sample rate, such as 96Khz, would recreate the sound wave digitally.

Analog Sound Wave   Sampling Process   Digital Sound Wave

A.

B.

C.

If sample rate is the number of snapshots of sound that are taken per second, then bit depth is the overall resolution of each one of those snapshots. We call it bit depth because it uses the binary system of bits, 1s and 0s, to define the amplitude of each sample your recorder records every second. The higher the bit depth, the more accurately your recorder is able to determine the amplitude of each sample it takes.

Professional CD audio uses 16-bit audio, which has 65,536 different values to define each sample's amplitude. Professional Blu-ray films, on the other hand, can be delivered in 24-bit audio, which has 16,777,216 values. As with sample rate, the higher the bit depth, the more storage space is required. When referring to the sample rate and bit depth of audio, professionals will describe it as 16/44.1 or 24/96 instead of writing out or saying 16-bit/44,100Hz or 24-bit/96,000Hz.

MP3 files are a compressed format that is typically measured in bit rate instead of sample rate and bit depth. MP3s range between 96-320Kb per second bit rates, with 160Kb per second being considered to be about the quality of a CD. CD audio is 16/44.1kHz. Professional audio is typically 24/48kHz or 24/96kHz.

If you are unsure of which sample rate and bit depth to use, try starting with 24/48kHz for professional audio. If you plan on being a professional sound effects producer one day, you might as well start right now. You can also experiment by recording at 24/96kHz and see if you can hear the difference when you play the sounds really slow in a process called "pitch-shifting." We'll talk more about that later.

MICROPHONE RECORDING LEVEL/INPUT LEVEL

The sensitivity of your microphone is controlled by the "microphone recording level." Some recorders have a fader, some have knobs, and some have switches. These

MAKE SOME NOISE VIERS

controls will allow you to change the level of the micro-phone that the recorder is recording.

HEADPHONE LEVELS

Most recorders have a knob or fader that allows you to con-trol the volume of your headphones. A good rule of thumb is to turn the volume off or as low as possible whenever you are putting your headphones on. Then, slowly raise the volume of your headphones. This will prevent your ears from being exposed to unexpectedly loud sounds.

Caution: Exposure to loud volumes will cause perma-nent damage to your ears. Always listen at a low to moderate volume.

MONO/STEREO

This selection allows you to decide if the file you are recording will be mono, which is one microphone or input being recorded to a single track, or stereo, which is two microphones or inputs being recorded to two sepa-rate tracks. If you are using both of the XLR inputs for an external stereo microphone or two mono microphones, then you should select "stereo." Also select "stereo" if you are using the on-board microphone on your hand-held recorder. If you are only using one XLR input for a mono microphone, then select "mono." When record-ing with a mono microphone most recorders use the "left" or "channel 1" input for mono sources.

Note: Some recorders allow you to record more than two channels of audio, but to keep things easier, we'll focus on mono and stereo recordings in this book.

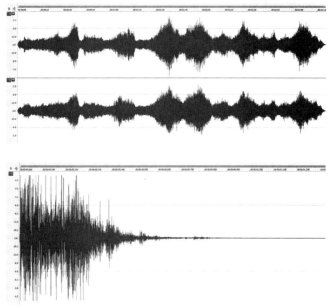

Top: Stereo File, Bottom: Mono File

INTERNAL SPEAKER

Many handheld and portable recorders offer the option to use a speaker inside the unit. This is useful for listening back to takes with friends, but always turn the internal speaker off when you are recording. Failure to do so could result in feedback. That said, if you hear feedback, be sure to record it.

RECORDING LEVELS

All recorded audio is measured in negative numbers. These numbers, also known as levels, will let you know if your recording is too quiet or too loud. The levels on your recorder show you the amplitude that the recorder is picking up from the sound being recorded. Almost every recorder measures sound in a range from -INF (which stands for negative infinity or absolute silence) to -0dBFS. dBFS, or "decibel full scale," is a special form of decibels used for measuring digital sound and is often only shown as "dB" on recorders. -0dBFS is the maximum amplitude a recorder can receive before it clips, which is an unflattering form of digital distortion. You always want your recordings to be under -0dB. Once a recording clips, the clipped section of audio is lost and is usually unable to be fixed, even with very expensive equipment.

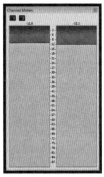

dBFS Meter

Every recorder is a little different on how the levels or meters work, but in general you want to try to keep most of your recordings within the -25dB to -10dB range, which visually would be 70% to 90% of the recording level bar. Adjust your recording levels by using the microphone level controls on your recorder.

Keep in mind; sounds that are naturally quiet like crickets chirping at night or a clock ticking might not reach this range. In some cases, they might not even reach -30 or -40dB. That's okay. Quiet sounds are meant to sound quiet. Record the best levels you can, but make sure to check the levels of your recordings so that you know that all your hard work doesn't go to waste.

■ HEADPHONES

Headphones come in all shapes and sizes and can range from as low as five dollars to hundreds of dollars. The best kind of headphones to use are ones that cover your entire ear. As a sound effects recordist, you want to hear what your microphone is recording just like a photographer wants to see the image they're taking as they line up their shot. Headphones that cover your entire ear do this best because they help block out other sounds from reaching your ears. There are also headphones like the Direct Sound EX-25 that reduce noise coming from outside the headphones to allow you to focus only on the sound that the headphones are producing.

Headphones

Earbuds can work in a pinch, but you'll hear your work better by using headphones that cover your ears. The speakers in headphones are also larger than earbuds, which means you will be able to hear more of the frequencies of what you're recording.

Note: No two pairs of headphones or speakers reproduce sound the same way. Professional headphones are designed to reproduce the sound as accurately as possible.

You don't have to spend a bunch of money for a great pair of headphones. The industry standard for headphones in the film business is the Sony MDR-7506 and they cost around $80. Try to avoid fancy consumer brand headphones that claim to enhance the sound. With these types of headphones, you won't accurately hear what you're actually recording because they alter the true sound in order to make it sound "better," plus you'll save a bunch of money.

LISTENING LEVELS

Listening to sounds or music through headphones at loud levels will damage your ears. Period. There is no way around this. You might think you'll be fine, but the world is full of aging rock stars and sound engineers who are now losing their hearing because of listening to their work at loud levels throughout their lives. If you enjoy recording and listening to music now, there's a good chance you'll want to do this when you're older. So, do your future self a favor and listen through your headphones at lower levels.

Unfortunately, there is no standard for headphone volume settings. Every recorder is different. Experiment with your recorder to find the best listening volume by starting at a low or no level and slowly increase the level until the volume is pleasant and not painful. Remember, when loud sounds happen unexpectedly your headphones will amplify them and you don't want to damage your hearing!

With these tips, a good pair of headphones and a handheld recorder, you're all set to begin recording sound effects.

— SEAN'S NOTES —

Overall, this chapter showed me the different types of equipment and the things that go into recording. Personally, I feel that it is good to work with what you have, but it is also important to have good gear. I love to go out with a handheld recorder and headphones and record whatever I can find. The simplicity of this allows me to use basic equipment and have fun recording without having to get too technical with the fancy gear. However, it is good to know your gear and how to properly use it when going out and recording.

 RECORDING AND PERFORMING SOUND EFFECTS

■ AUTONOMOUS SOUND VS. PERFORMED SOUND

There are two types of sounds that you will record when making sound effects. The first type of sound is autonomous sound. Autonomous sound is a fancy of way of saying that the sound controls itself and you are there to record whatever happens with little or no control over the sound that is produced. Examples of autonomous sounds are birds chirping, planes flying overhead, and traffic. The second type of sound is performed sound. Performed sound is a sound that you have control over and therefore can manipulate to give you the results you're after. Examples of performed sounds include opening/closing doors, running water in the sink, and turning things off and on. With performed sounds, you get to control what happens, when it happens, how it happens and how long it happens. Let's go over both types of sounds in further detail.

AUTONOMOUS SOUND

Autonomous sounds can be challenging to record because you have no control over what happens or even when it happens, so you have to be ready for whatever happens—whenever it happens. Some recorders have a pre-record function that allows the recorder to continuously record and save a certain number of seconds of audio in temporary storage before you hit the record button. Once you press the record button and start the actual recording, the take begins however many seconds before you pressed record that your recorder's pre-record function is set to. Pre-record times differ per unit, so be sure to check your user manual. The pre-record function is a great way to ensure that you don't miss any part of a sound that you weren't planning on hearing (for example, a plane flying overhead). Keep in mind, using the pre-record function will drain battery life from your recorder because the unit is continuously recording.

When recording autonomous sound, it is very important to remain alert to your surroundings so you don't miss anything. But, just because you can't control the sound doesn't mean you can't plan to record the sound. Here are some examples of autonomous sounds and how to plan to record them:

- *Airplanes*
- *Birds*
- *Crickets*
- *Neighborhood Ambiences*
- *School Bus Stop Ambiences*
- *Weather*

AIRPLANES

Airplanes are difficult to plan for unless you know their flight patterns and flight schedules. Having this information helps you plan for when you might have a chance to record the airplanes flying overhead. If you desperately need airplanes, you could travel to the airport and find a place to record that is outside of the airport, but close to the runway. Granted, you can't control the airplanes or direct them on how and where to fly, but you can plan to be near the action.

BIRDS

Birds always seem to chirp until you start recording. Then, it seems they fly away or decide to get quiet until you start recording something else, which is usually when they start chirping again. If you want to record birds, your best bet is to record them when they want to chirp the most. This usually happens in the early parts of the morning before or just as the sun is rising as well as in the evening right around when the sun is setting.

CRICKETS

Unlike birds, once crickets start chirping, they don't stop. The best time to record crickets is at night when they are the most active. If possible, you can catch a cricket and bring the insect indoors to a quiet place to record. With enough single chirps, you can edit them together and make them sound like an entire forest full of crickets.

NEIGHBORHOOD AMBIENCES

Neighborhood ambiences are full of kids playing, dogs barking, lawnmowers, and sprinklers. Getting everyone in the neighborhood together to reenact these sounds can be frustrating, if not impossible. However, you can plan to record when these sounds normally happen. Most people in the neighborhood are at school or work during the week, so the weekend is usually the best time to record the sound of your neighborhood. You might not get all of the sounds you want to happen when you want them to happen in your recording, but you can always edit and combine really long takes together to make a custom sound effect that has all the sounds you're after.

SCHOOL BUS STOP AMBIENCES

If you're after the sound of kids getting off a school bus, you'll need to plan on being at the bus stop a little early to set up your recorder. Position the microphone on the same side of the street where the school bus will arrive and open its doors. If it's obvious that you're recording, kids are more likely to stop and ask what you are doing. Unfortunately, these questions will end up in your recording. The sound of kids getting off a school bus and asking, "Hey, what are you doing?" or "Is that a microphone?" is not very useful. So, try to position your recorder in an inconspicuous place that's not easily noticeable, like in a nearby bush or on top of a mailbox pointed at the bus stop. If you only want the sound of the school bus passing by, position the microphone further up the street so that you can hear the bus pass by long enough before it stops at the bus stop. This way, you get the sound of the bus without the kids laughing and talking at the bus stop.

WEATHER

Weather is probably the most unpredictable autonomous sound to record, because even the weatherman doesn't know for sure when thunderstorms will happen. They make good guesses, but they never know for certain. If you need to record weather sounds like rain, have your gear ready when a storm is approaching. The best place to record rain is inside your garage with the garage door open. This protects the recording equipment from getting wet, but still allows your microphone to capture the sound of the rain.

Rainfall is basically the sound of water drops on a surface. If you have a cement driveway, you'll hear the sound of water drops on cement. If you have a dirt driveway, then you'll hear the sound of water drops on dirt. If there is a car in the driveway outside of the garage, you will hear the sound of water drops on the car as well as the surface of the driveway.

A good way to recreate the sound of rain is to use a hose with a sprinkler or fountain attachment and record the sound of the water on various surfaces. The recording can be looped and layered to make the hose sound like a torrential downpour or the soft splattering of rain.

PERFORMED SOUND

How good a sound effect sounds largely relies on how well the sound was performed. Performed sounds can offer the best recordings for sound effects because you have total control over the sound. The art of performing sound effects gets its roots from the movie business in a process called Foley recording.

JACK FOLEY

The name Foley comes from Jack Foley who is famous for pioneering the art of Foley during his work at Universal Pictures during the 1930s. The stage that he worked on was specifically used for recreating sounds for the movies Universal Pictures was producing and since it was his workroom, people referred to the room as "Foley's stage." The name Foley stage stuck and today, nearly every major post-production audio house uses a Foley stage to recreate sound for on-screen action.

Professional Foley stages are soundproofed to block out any sound coming from outside the room. The room is acoustically treated to eliminate reverberation from sounds generated inside the room. The floor of the stage is usually designed with different surfaces built into the floor to perform on such as wood, marble, concrete, carpet, and even dirt! Since Foley work is performed while watching a movie, there is usually a large television or even a movie screen located on the stage.

As the sound effects industry grew during the turn of the 21st century, sound effects recordists began to rely on Foley practices when recording in the field to help them produce interesting and useful Foley sound effects outside of the Foley stage, including sounds that were traditionally recorded while watching action on a screen. Foley sound effects are incredibly important to a movie, TV show, or video game and having these types of sounds in your library will help you produce better sounding productions.

THE ART OF FOLEY

Foley relies heavily on finding the sound or "voice" of an object. There are several methods used to find this such as rubbing, twisting, turning, bending, sliding, shaking, dropping, and even breaking (with permission) the object. Be sure to listen to the sound with your ears and not with your eyes, because the audience will never *see* how you recorded something, but they will *hear* how it sounds. Just because an object looks interesting doesn't mean it will sound interesting.

The props used during a Foley session are critical to how good the sound effects will sound. Foley artists (the name given to people who perform Foley) will often collect and store hundreds of sound props to use. Each prop is used for a specific sound or sometimes a bunch of different sounds, but the secret to finding a good prop is to *listen* to the prop. You'll be surprised what items can be used for props. Remember to use your imagination!

Here's a list of common props found on a Foley Stage and what they can be used for:

ANALOG TAPE OR CELLOPHANE STRIPS

The thin plastic texture of these objects creates a very convincing grass surface to walk on.

CELLOPHANE SHEETS

Using cellophane sheets for crackling fire is an old Foley trick that dates all the way back to the early Walt Disney cartoons.

COCONUTS

Coconuts are probably the most commonly known props used in Foley. When a coconut is split in half and the fruit is removed, the two halves can be used for the clippity-clop sound of horse hooves.

Recording Coconut Shells for Horse Hooves

CORNSTARCH

Cornstarch can be used for a believable snow surface to walk on. Many Foley artists have spent a sunny day in California walking on the snowy surfaces of cornstarch. It's almost a Hollywood tradition.

FRUITS AND VEGETABLES

Nearly all of the blood and gore that you hear in big blockbuster Hollywood movies is created using various fruits and vegetables for their crunches, squishes, and splats. Here's a short list of some of the most common fruits and vegetables used in Foley:

APPLE

Apples are great for the classic bite or chomp sound. Simply hold the apple close to the microphone and take a big bite.

CABBAGE

Cabbage leaves have a nice crunch to them, especially when several leaves are twisted together, but one of the best uses for cabbage is for head drops. When an actor says "Off with their head," reach for the cabbage!

CELERY

Twisting a stalk of celery creates a very realistic bone break. For the best results, twist several stalks together.

MELON

Head drops can also be created with melons, but with the added benefit of a juicier impact from the flesh and juice inside. After a few drops, the melon usually splits open. Continue to record the drops and try a few takes by dropping the melon flesh-side down for some good splats.

ORANGE

Oranges can make for great squishes when cut in half and squeezed.

WATERMELON

Watermelons are great for stabbing, dropping, and even scooping out the flesh to create juicy blood splats.

Vegetables to be used for punches, splats and bone breaks!

Note: When working with fruits and vegetables, it's a good idea to have extra garbage bags and towels to help you clean up the mess. Be sure to use some form of wind protection to keep all of the fruit guts off the microphone.

HOT WATER BOTTLE

Filling a hot water bottle with air and scraping the bottle against a smooth surface like a countertop or clean cement floor will create a very realistic tire screeching sound.

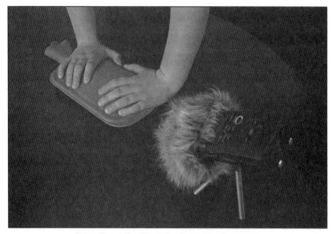

Recording a Hot Water Bottle for Tire Screeches

NEWSPAPER

Smacking rolls of newspaper together or hitting them with your fist can make hard-hitting punches. You can also strike the newspaper against surfaces like leather coats or an old leather couch for a fleshier sound.

ROCK SALT

Walking on rock salt creates a realistic gravel texture and can be used to help footsteps have more grit.

RUSTY HINGES

Hinges are great for metal squeaks. The secret is to make sure the hinge is rusty. If you don't have a rusty hinge, you can leave a hinge in a bucket of water outside for a few months or even a year to create the rust.

SHOES

Footsteps are a staple Foley sound effect. Some Foley artists will have dozens of pairs of shoes to choose from for the perfect sound of the character's footsteps. If you find a great sounding pair of shoes, but they're not your size, try putting the shoes on your hands to perform the action.

STAPLE GUN

Guns are expensive and potentially dangerous, especially when dropped! A safe and less destructive way to record the sound of a gun being dropped is to use a metal staple gun.

STRAW

Blowing through a straw into a glass of water makes the perfect sound of bubbles. The deeper the straw goes into the water the deeper the sound will be. How hard you blow into the straw also affects the sound.

STRAW BROOM

The bristles on a straw broom can be used to mimic leaf movements for rustling foliage.

WOOD DOWEL RODS

Swinging a wood dowel rod in front of a microphone gives a great whip or whoosh sound. How fast you swing the dowel, as well as its length and width, affects the sound.

Recording a Dowel Rod

This is just a short list of the thousands of props that Foley artists use in their craft. A good Foley artist will have a collection of personal props that they've collected over the years. Start building your prop collection by asking friends and family as well as looking through the recycling bin, and checking out places like dollar stores, thrift shops, flea markets, and garage sales. Avoid throwing anything away without asking yourself if it can be used to make noise. This will help you get into the practice of listening to objects and give you an arsenal of sound to play with. You'll be surprised at how fast your prop collection will grow.

TIPS ON PERFORMING SOUND EFFECTS

What you are recording will make a bigger impact on the final sound than *how* you record it. If the sound source is lame, the sound effect will probably be lame. Technical aspects of the sound can be fixed, but performance is very difficult and in some cases impossible to fix. Get the best sound source and the best performance first, then worry about the technical stuff.

Here are some tips for performing sound:

MOVES LIKE JAGGER!

Just about everything makes sound. It all comes down to how you perform with the object. Certain objects can make really cool squeaks, creaks and moans, but only if you move, twist, rotate, bend or otherwise stress the object in unimaginable ways. Spend time experimenting with your prop to see what sounds you can make with it. It's a great idea to record while you experiment in case you make an interesting sound that you might not be able to reproduce. Doors and other hinged objects are notorious for losing their squeak after a few performances. Play it safe and make sure you're recording whenever you're making noise.

HOLD YOUR BREATH!

Pay close attention to your breathing. While you are used to the sound of your breath, the microphone hears it loud and clear. Breathing during a take, especially while recording quiet material, will cause your breath to be heard during the recording. A common trick is to hold your breath during the take. Use slow, shallow breaths for longer takes that require you to breathe. Also, breathing through your mouth can sometimes be quieter than breathing through your nose.

WEAR QUIET CLOTHES!

Even though parachute pants have been out of style for over thirty years, there are still some noisy fabrics that are still in fashion today. Wear quiet clothes that don't jingle or make excessive noise when you move. The same advice goes for jewelry. Rings, long necklaces, and dangly earrings can all make noise when you move or handle props. If you can hear your clothes while you're performing, so can the microphone.

WATCH YOUR STEP!

Be aware of the sound of your footsteps during takes that require you to move. Take your shoes off and wear only socks when you need to record something that you need to walk with, especially if the mic is near your feet (e.g. rolling luggage). Even when you are not walking, your feet can make a sound when you shift your weight during a take. Tread lightly.

LOCATION, LOCATION, LOCATION!

Where you place the microphone will make a huge difference in how the recording sounds. Pointing the microphone toward the direction of the sound is not the same as recording the source of the sound. For example, you can point your microphone at a door when it opens, but technically the door isn't making the sound. Instead, the sound is created by the squeaks that the hinges make while the door opens. So, you want to point the microphone at the hinges, which are the source of the sound.

The sound source is the exact place where the sound waves are being generated. Experiment with your microphone placement to determine which position *sounds* the best. Be sure to listen with your *ears* and not with your *eyes*. For sound sources that are difficult to locate, a good trick is to close your eyes and focus only on what you hear. Move the microphone around the area and find the sweet spot that makes the sound come alive.

CLOSE ENOUGH!

In general, it's a good idea to get the microphone as close to the sound source as possible. This will reduce the amount of background noise and you won't have to use as much microphone gain on the recorder, which will make your recording cleaner.

If you position the microphone too close to the sound source, you get a phenomenon called the "proximity effect." This effect causes the microphone to artificially increase the low frequencies that results in a bassy sound. For voices, the proximity effect helps the voice sound richer and fuller, while for other sources it can produce a muddy sound. Moving the microphone a few inches away from the sound source will eliminate this effect. For more information about the art of Foley, I highly recommend the book *The Foley Grail* by my friend and Foley artist Vanessa Theme Ament.

Vanessa Theme Ament and Ric Viers

— SEAN'S NOTES —

How you perform and record the sound is just as important as the equipment that you use. How you perform with the object can change the sound that it produces. In the past, my dad and I have done some pretty fun things in Foley, from smashing TVs to recording weapons, and I've had a blast.

CHAPTER 4

THE TEN RECORDING COMMANDMENTS

I n my book *The Sound Effects Bible*, I created a list of Ten Recording Commandments to follow when recording sound effects. This list is used by professionals all over the world and will help you prepare for your recording sessions and record better sound.

Warning! If you break any of these commandments, you might not end up with good recordings.

■ TEN RECORDING COMMANDMENTS

1. Thou Shalt Have a Pre-Roll and Post-Roll of Two Seconds on Each Recording
2. Thou Shalt Record More Than You Need
3. Thou Shalt Slate Every Take with as Much Information as Possible

4. Thou Shalt Check Thy Levels Often

5. Thou Shalt Listen to Thy Work by Always Wearing Headphones

6. Thou Shalt Eliminate All Background Noise

7. Thou Shalt Not Interrupt a Take

8. Thou Shalt Point the Microphone at the Sound

9. Thou Shalt Check Thy Equipment Before Going into the Field

10. Thou Shalt Remember the Copyright Laws to Keep Them Unbroken

1. THOU SHALT HAVE A PRE-ROLL AND POST-ROLL OF TWO SECONDS ON EACH RECORDING

Back in the days of analog tape recorders, the recorder would begin to "roll" the tape in order to record the sound. Today, recorders are digital and no tape is actually used; however, it is still common practice on professional movie sets to say "roll sound" when you want the sound mixer to start recording. When you record sound effects, you will want to "roll" your recorder for a couple of seconds before you begin to perform or capture your sound. This is known as pre-roll. Pre-roll ensures that the recorder is recording because sometimes it takes the recorder a moment to actually start recording after you've pressed the record button.

Some recorders make you press the record button twice (the first time only puts the recorder in pause mode) before it will start recording. A good tip is to check the counter on the recorder's display to make sure that the numbers are moving to guarantee that the recorder is recording. Additionally, giving the recorder a couple of seconds before you start to perform or capture sound allows you to settle down and get quiet. You don't want to hear yourself moving around during the sound after you've pressed record.

Some people like to record a new take for each sound that they are recording. Other people will continue to record several objects in a room or location and simply slate what each new sound is in the same take. You can create a marker in the audio file on most recorders. If not, you can clap or snap your fingers near the microphone to give an audible cue as well as a visible spike in the waveform of the audio file before slating the next sound action. Each technique has an advantage. Using a different take for each sound you record keeps things organized and easier to find when you are editing your sound, but recording multiple sounds in the same take allows you to work faster. Both techniques are perfectly acceptable, so experiment and see which technique works best for your recording style.

Post-roll is the process of allowing the recorder to continue recording for a couple of seconds after the desired sound is finished. Allowing a couple of seconds to pass after the sound has happened ensures that the sound has finished completely. This is important because sometimes you might think the sound is finished but there is still reverb from the room in the recording or the item you are recording is still settling (for example, the ringing sound of metal from a pot that you drop on the ground). You want to make sure that the sound is completely finished before you stop your recording. This also eliminates the chance of self-noise (the noise coming from you when you move to press stop on the recorder) from messing up your otherwise perfect sound.

2. THOU SHALT RECORD MORE THAN YOU NEED

Recording more material than you need (also called over-recording) is a good habit to form. You never really know how good something sounds until you listen to it back in a quiet environment. There might be a noise in the background or something else that you didn't notice. If you record multiple takes, you have a better chance of recording a clean take.

Even if you only need the sound of a door closing once, it's a great idea to record several takes and decide which one you like later. When recording multiple takes of a sound, try recording a few extra sounds that are different from one another. For example, close the door softly, then close the door harder, then slam the door. Now you have a variety of different performances from the same object. This will help you build up your own personal library of sound effects with a variety of performances to choose from. You'll thank me later.

3. THOU SHALT SLATE EVERY TAKE WITH AS MUCH INFORMATION AS POSSIBLE

Slating is the process of recording your voice on the take to identify what you are recording. This is extremely important! While you might convince yourself that you'll remember everything you recorded, you will be surprised how many times you'll listen back to your recordings and have no idea what you are listening to.

When slating, it's helpful to include as much information about what you are recording as you can. If you are recording the sound of a door opening/closing, then include details such as type of door, location of the door, etc. For example, you might say "Wooden bedroom door opening and closing." This will help you remember what you recorded and also give you useful information when naming the sound later.

4. THOU SHALT CHECK THY LEVELS OFTEN

Always keep an eye on the levels of your recorder. If the levels weren't recorded properly, you might have to do it all over again or settle for poor quality sound. If you're not watching your levels while you record, you might not realize that the recording is bad until later on when you edit or listen to your recordings.

Also, every sound is different and you may have to adjust your levels or microphone placement to account for this. It's a good idea to double check your levels before you record and glance back at your levels periodically during the recording, especially when the volume of the sound is noticeably different. If it sounds louder in your headphones, then it will record at higher levels on the recorder.

It's a good idea to wait until the sound is finished before you change your levels. Changing levels in the middle of a take will mean that the sound will go up and down in the recording. You can always try to fix levels that weren't perfect, but if you're in the middle of recording a sound and the levels aren't really bad, wait until the sound is over and try recording again at better levels. You never know; that take might end up being usable anyways. If you are recording something that you only get one shot at recording (for example, a random helicopter flying overhead), then you should adjust your levels, but only do this if you have to. The levels don't need to be perfect, just in a good range.

5. THOU SHALT LISTEN TO THY WORK BY ALWAYS WEARING HEADPHONES

It doesn't make sense to take pictures without looking at the screen or viewfinder of the camera. You might not have the picture in focus or there might be things in the background that you don't want to be in the picture. In the same way, it doesn't make sense to record sound without listening to what you are recording. This is the purpose of always wearing headphones.

Headphones allow you to monitor what the microphone is hearing. This is very useful when deciding where to point the microphone or finding out what sounds are in the background that you need to get rid of. For example, you might not notice a clock ticking while standing in the room, but when you put your headphones on and listen you can hear the clock along with other things that you might not normally notice.

But it's more than noticing what shouldn't be there. I like to wear my headphones throughout the recording session even if I'm not recording because there are times when I'll notice sounds I might not have otherwise noticed just when walking around. Get into the practice of always wearing your headphones. Never assume that what your ears hear is what your microphone hears.

6. THOU SHALT ELIMINATE ALL BACKGROUND NOISE

Background noise is the enemy of good sound. This is why recording studios will spend hundreds of thousands of dollars to build soundproof rooms to record in. They are trying to eliminate any sound that shouldn't be in the recording. Field recording is a challenge because most of the time you have to go where the sound is and the sound is rarely in a quiet, noise-free environment. So, you'll need to do your best to eliminate all of the background noise that you can.

The challenge with recording in your house while other family members are home is that they can get annoyed or inconvenienced by your request for long periods of silence. If possible, try recording at times when family members are away, outside, or occupied with quiet activities like reading. If you have a sibling that wants to watch television or play a video game, ask if they would mind doing so with headphones.

If you find something really cool to record, but the environment or room is really noisy, try taking the object to a quiet location to record. If the object can't be moved, you'll need to reduce the background noise. There are four types of background noise that you need to be aware of:

1. Constant Noise
2. Periodic Noise
3. Intermittent Noise
4. Random Noise

CONSTANT NOISE

Constant noises are sounds that are always heard in the background. Here are some examples of constant noises and solutions for them:

FLUORESCENT LIGHTS FLICKERING OR BALLAST HUM

If you're working in a pole barn or garage that has noisy fluorescent lights, try turning them off and working with another light source.

FANS

Fans can usually be turned off, but if they need to be on for a reason, check to see if it's okay to temporarily turn them off.

HIGHWAY TRAFFIC

Highway traffic is a constant flow of vehicles on the road. During rush hour or peak drive times, there are rarely noticeable gaps in between the passing cars because there are no traffic lights to control the flow of traffic. The resulting sound is a steady hum of cars.

TICKING CLOCKS

Ticking clocks are typically battery powered and can be disabled by removing the battery, but don't forget to adjust the time when you plug the battery back in!

PERIODIC NOISE

Periodic noises are sounds that are part of your recording environment which happen at regular and often predictable times. Here are some examples of periodic noises and solutions for them:

CLOCK CHIMES

Clock chimes are predictable because they happen every hour or sometimes every fifteen minutes. If you can't disable the clock (for example, an antique grandfather clock that is wound up with no "off" setting), try timing your takes in between the chimes. Be aware of the time though, so you don't spoil a take!

STREET TRAFFIC

Street traffic occurs at intervals due to traffic lights controlling the flow of traffic. With street traffic, you can sometimes time your takes in between the group of cars that are passing when the light turns green.

TORNADO SIRENS

In the United States, it's a common practice for cities to test their emergency sirens on the first Saturday of every month at 1pm. As a result, I avoid recording outdoors and sometimes indoors at that time. Granted, the tests usually only last for a few minutes, but you should be aware of similar tests in your area so you don't have something elaborate planned only to be ruined by a blaring siren.

TRAINS

If you live in an area near train tracks, try to locate a train schedule. You can search online or check with your local township office to see if they can supply you with one to determine the best time to record. If you want to record train horns, try standing near an intersection. This is where trains usually blow their horns to alert drivers of their crossing.

Caution: Never go on the train tracks! Stay a minimum of fifteen feet away from the tracks. Trains are loud, so there is no reason to risk your safety when you can safely record them from a safer distance. If you have a backyard that is located next to the train tracks, stay in your yard.

INTERMITTENT NOISE

Intermittent noises are sounds that are part of your recording environment that happen at non-regular intervals. In some cases the sound will repeat after a period of time, but there is no way of telling when it will repeat. Here are some examples of intermittent noises and solutions for them:

AIR CONDITIONING UNITS

Air conditioning units are triggered by a thermostat, which turns the air conditioner on when the thermostat reaches a specific temperature. You can turn the unit off or simply raise the thermostat level. Be sure to put the thermostat back to the original setting once you're done.

AIR TRAFFIC

Airplanes, jets and helicopters are not good friends of sound recordists, unless of course you are recording them. Depending on where you live, most air traffic is sporadic and you might have to deal with a plane flying overhead and ruining a take now and then. If you live near the airport, you've probably gotten used to the sounds of airplanes flying overhead. Unfortunately, this will be a problem for recording sound effects. Some airports alternate approach and landing patterns by switching which runways are used during certain times of the day. For example, in the morning, incoming flights might come from the south, but alternate to the north during the afternoon. Pay attention to these flight patterns to see if you can find a window of time to record without air traffic.

FURNACES

Furnaces can be handled in the same way as air conditioners, by either turning them off or by changing the thermostat level. Note that unlike air conditioning units, sometimes a furnace will take a few minutes to shut down, so be patient until the unit is off before you record.

GAMING SYSTEM FANS

If you have a gaming system that is still running even though the television may be off, be aware that the fan may turn on periodically to cool down the unit. If you plan on recording in the same room as the gaming system, it would be best to turn the system off completely to avoid this.

REFRIGERATORS

Compressors on refrigerators are similar to air conditioning units in that they turn on at a certain temperature to keep the groceries cold. If you plan on recording in the kitchen, you should turn off the refrigerator. Of course, the challenge here is remembering to turn the refrigerator back on when you're done recording or your parents might be upset at all of the spoiled food. A good trick to remember to turn the refrigerator back on is to place your car keys in the refrigerator. This way you'll remember to turn the refrigerator back on before you leave. If you don't drive yet or you're working from home, try leaving your cell phone in the refrigerator. You can live without the internet for a few minutes.

SUMP PUMPS

Most basements have a sump pump which pumps out water from underneath the foundation. Depending on where your sump pump is located, this could be heard throughout the house. If you plan on recording in the basement, you may hear the sump pump running periodically. The pump usually only lasts for a minute or two, so you'll have to work around this by covering the pump with some blankets or pausing your session until the sump pump turns off. *It is strongly advised that you do not turn off the sump pump. Failure to turn the pump back on could result in a flooded basement, which could mean the end of your recording career at home.*

POTENTIAL NOISE

Potential noises are sounds that could happen at any time but are not happening when you start your recording session. Potential noises can be entirely random or later discovered to be periodic or intermittent noises within that environment. Here are some examples of potential noises and solutions for them:

DOGS BARKING

Animals are fun to have, but they make noise at the most inconvenient times. If you have a rambunctious animal, put them outside or in another room to avoid barks and scampering feet in your recordings. If they still bark when they're outside, try giving them a treat or a toy to keep them occupied.

DOORBELLS

Ding-dong! That's the sound of a good take getting ruined. If you want to avoid the doorbell going off while you record, try placing a note on the door or, even better, over the doorbell to let people know you are recording.

DOORS OPENING

Professional studios have a red light outside the room to let people know when recording is taking place. Instead of a fancy light, you can use the same strategy as the doorbell by placing a sticky note on the door to inform people that you are in the room recording. This is a good idea if you are setting up recording equipment on the other side of the door.

PHONES RINGING

Phones are ticking time bombs to a sound effects recordist. The only problem is you never know when they are going to go off. So, if possible and you have permission, turn off the ringer for the phone or disconnect the phone. This will give you a ring-free environment to record in.

TOILET FLUSHES

Everybody poops. Everyone knows this. It's just science! However, a toilet flush can cause a good take to go down the drain. Pun intended. To avoid not only a toilet flush but a long minute or two of running water as the toilet tank refills in the middle of your recording, try placing a note on the bathroom door or toilet asking people if they wouldn't mind waiting to use the bathroom until after you're finished recording. Keep in mind; when you gotta go, you gotta go.

7. THOU SHALT NOT INTERRUPT A TAKE

Takes are filled with great sounds, OK sounds, bad sounds, mistakes and happy accidents. That's all part of the joy of recording. Sometimes you never know what you're going to get. You'll end up with some cool material if you remember to stay quiet during the take, regardless of what happens. I've recorded some "mistakes" that turned out to be happy accidents that were usable and even better than what I was trying to record.

If something goes wrong that isn't dangerous, let it happen and see what you get! A lot of times, you won't know what you have recorded until after the session when you are listening back to your work. So, avoid talking, moving, or trying to fix the mistake because once you do, the take will be unusable. That said, if you accidentally hurt yourself or set fire to the living room rug, then by all means, stop the take.

Moving the microphone while recording can also spoil a take. In some cases, you may want to move the microphone to follow a sound that is passing by or to create a really cool effect with the microphone. For normal recording, it's a great practice to keep the microphone in one position to avoid phasing problems, slight changes in pitch, wind noise/air movement and other issues. Movement during stereo recordings like ambiences will cause the stereo image to shift, which sounds unnatural. If you need to pan the sound for a scene, you are better off doing the panning during editing than recording the pan with the microphone. A microphone stand is the best solution for recording ambiences because it will allow you to record for long periods of time without worrying about your arms getting tired.

Using a Mini Tripod as a Stand for a Handheld Recorder

8. THOU SHALT POINT THE MICROPHONE AT THE SOUND

Where you point or place your microphone is called Microphone Placement. Microphone placement is perhaps the single most deciding factor in how good your recording will be. If the microphone is too far away, the sound will either sound distant or if you are indoors, the sound might sound echoey from the reverb of the room (reverb is the result of sound waves bouncing off walls). Also, simply pointing a microphone toward an object doesn't mean that's the best position for the microphone.

If you're struggling to decide where to point the microphone, just use your ears. With your headphones on, point the microphone at different parts of the object or location that you are recording and find the spot that sounds the best to you. Experiment and have fun with this. It's your recording. It should sound the way you want it to sound. Don't be afraid to try crazy things. That's part of the fun!

9. THOU SHALT CHECK THY EQUIPMENT BEFORE GOING INTO THE FIELD

Field recording is the name given to recording sessions that take place outside of the studio, or in your case, outside of your home. The main thing to remember when recording in the field is to make sure that you have all of your gear and plenty of batteries. Nothing is more frustrating than getting all your gear set up and realizing that your batteries are dead or that you forgot your headphones or you didn't reformat the card that you are recording to. Every good recording session starts by checking your gear and making sure that everything works and that you didn't forget anything. You don't want to stop your recording session because you need to go home for something you forgot.

Here's a list of things to check before you start recording:

1. Did you transfer the data from the recorder from the previous session?
2. Did you format the internal storage or memory card?
3. Did you set up your recorder to the right settings (e.g. mono/stereo, sample rate/bit depth, etc.)?
4. If you're using an external microphone, does it need phantom power?
5. Do you have your headphones, including any necessary adaptors?
6. Do you have fresh batteries?

7. Do you have spare batteries?

8. Do you have a spare memory card?

Asking yourself these questions will ensure that you have everything you need and are ready to start recording!

And since we're talking about recording in the field, here's an A to Z list of ideas for places to record:

- Amusement Park
- Beach
- Camping
- Downtown Area
- Equestrian Ranch
- Farms
- Grocery Store
- Hotels
- Ice Rink
- Junkyard
- Karate Dojo
- Lake
- Mall
- Nature Center
- Offices
- Parades
- Quiet Locations
- Restaurant
- School Events
- Train Station
- Underpass
- Varsity Football
- Water Park
- X-Game Events

Ric Viers and Detroit Chop Shop interns recording in a mine shaft
deep below the surface of the earth!

Note: Always get permission to enter before recording in a building or private property.

10. THOU SHALT REMEMBER THE COPYRIGHT LAWS TO KEEP THEM UNBROKEN

If you're going to use your sound effects in a movie or post them on YouTube, you need to make sure that you don't have any copyrighted material in your sound effect. Any sound or music that is already in a movie soundtrack, television show, video game or music album is considered to be copyrighted material. You need to have permission to use this material and that's a very long and expensive process. So, make sure that if you're recording sound effects at a place like the fair, that you can't hear any music in the background, especially if you want to sell your sound effects one day!

— SEAN'S NOTES —

I found that the Ten Recording Commandments are very beneficial when you are planning to record. These are very important and should become a part of your regular routine. In my house, breaking one of these commandments results in my father disowning me. I'm just kidding! But seriously, bad things happen. So make sure you follow these commandments as your sound effects religion.

CHAPTER 5

RECORDING SESSIONS

■ PREPARING FOR A RECORDING SESSION

A recording session is a time dedicated to recording new material. How you manage your recording sessions is entirely up to you, but having a game plan before you get started can help maximize your time during the session. The best way to make good use of your time recording is to plan ahead.

There are four methods to consider for your recording session:

- Mission List
- Scavenger List
- Experimenting
- Exploring

MISSION LIST

A mission list recording session is a session dedicated to recording specific sound effects. For example, if you are working on an action-packed video that includes a fistfight, you're going to need punches, kicks, and other specific sound effects. Start by making a list of the sound effects you need. It helps to make two columns. In the first column, write the names of the sound effects that you need. In the second column, write the props or objects needed to create those sounds.

Making sure that you have all of the necessary props and objects before you pull out your recording gear can be a big time saver, and is especially valuable if you have a limited time to record your sound effects. Preparing for your sessions helps things go smoothly and efficiently. It can also spark creative ideas that you might not have thought of without spending the time to plan for the session.

SCAVENGER LIST

A scavenger list is like a mission list, but not as detailed. Sometimes you need types of sound effects, but you're not sure exactly what specific sound effects you want to record. The solution is to make a list of anything that you can think of that will be fun and useful in your project. With this type of list, you don't need to be specific. Columns with sound effects and props are helpful, but not necessary for a scavenge list session because you don't *have* to record all of the sounds. The mission list is complete when you've checked off your list, but a scavenger list is done whenever you've run out of ideas (or batteries).

The whiteboard at the Detroit Chop Shop with ideas for sound effects to record

EXPERIMENTING SESSIONS

Experimenting sessions usually have an objective, such as testing a new microphone or trying a new sound prop that you're making. Be sure to slate your takes for each experiment and give as much detail as possible for when you review the recordings later.

I perform different experiments depending on what type of gear I am testing. Whenever I get a new recorder, I like to perform experiments with the input levels to see how well the recorder works and to see what are the optimal settings for the recording levels. To do this, I like to record the same microphone at the same distance recording the same sound, but at different input levels on the recorder. For example, I might record four different takes with each take being 25% higher in level each time. The first take is at 25%, the second take is at 50%, the third take is at 75%, and the fourth take is at 100%. This lets me know the level that sounds the best with the least amount of noise from the recorder's microphone preamp. I also like to record silence with the microphone at different levels. This helps me understand where the recorder's microphone preamp becomes noticeably noisy on the level settings.

When I test microphones, I like to experiment with their polar pattern to see how wide the pattern is and where I should position the microphone when recording. Sometimes I'll do what is called a "microphone shootout." A microphone shootout is placing more than one microphone in the same position at the same recording level and recording the same sound. When you playback the recordings and listen to each microphone by itself, you can determine which microphone you like the best. This can be very helpful when deciding which microphone you want to buy or use for your next recording session.

EXPLORING SESSIONS

Exploring sessions are when you don't have anything specific that you need to record, but you still have an urge to record. This can lead to new ideas and sounds you may not have thought of. Sometimes it's a good idea to just grab your recording gear and see what you can find to record. I highly recommend exploring sessions because they not only make you a better sound recordist, but they also help you find sounds you may not have otherwise recorded. Recording sessions without an agenda to follow can be fun!

■ WRAPPING UP FROM A RECORDING SESSION

When you're done recording, you're not really done recording. Pressing the "stop" button doesn't mean you're finished for the day.

Here's a quick overview of things to do when wrapping up a recording session:

1. Transfer Recordings
2. Back Up Recordings
3. Check Your Batteries
4. Clean Up!
5. Put Gear Away

TRANSFER RECORDINGS

The most important thing you can do when you're finished recording is transferring your files to your computer. Don't skip this step even if you're exhausted or don't feel like it. Skipping this step could mean the accidental loss of your recordings. You're not finished with your recording session until your takes have been safely transferred.

BACK UP RECORDINGS

Two copies of your work are better than one. Having more than one copy of your recordings will protect you from losing your work. I recommend storing files in at least two different locations. This could be your computer's internal hard drive and a secondary storage medium such as a second internal hard drive, portable hard drive, USB stick, DVD or anything else that won't be affected if your computer died.

CHECK YOUR BATTERIES

If you're using rechargeable batteries, don't forget to recharge the batteries so that you're ready for your next recording session. Charging batteries can take a few hours, so it's best to let them charge when you're not recording, rather than waiting around to record because you have to recharge your batteries. If you're using disposable batteries, replace the used batteries with fresh ones. In general, I recommend only recording with fresh batteries to avoid losing power in the middle of a recording session. If you're on a tight budget, you can try squeezing another recording session out of the used batteries, but be sure to have fresh spare batteries on hand. If you're not sure how much life your batteries have, you can purchase a battery tester at your local electronics store to check your batteries.

CLEAN UP!

Clean up is never fun, but it's necessary, especially if someone let you use their place or things to record. Be courteous and return everything the way it was when you started. People will be more likely to let you borrow or use their things if they know that you'll be responsible and return them the way you found them. Double check everything you turned off or on, store things where they came from and make sure you have all of your gear. And finally, don't forget to check the fridge!

PUT GEAR AWAY

Taking care of your recording equipment will help your gear last longer. If you take care of your gear, your gear will take care of you. Find a case or at least a box to store your equipment. Bags can be used, but they don't really protect the gear. It's a good idea to use something sturdier in case it's dropped or something falls on it. The last thing you want to happen is for someone to accidentally step on your recording equipment because it wasn't put away properly.

Cables are perhaps the most challenging item to put away because cables love to be messy and bunched up into knots. Not only are these knots difficult to untie when you need to lengthen the cable, but they can also cause the cable to go bad because of the strain it puts on the fragile wires inside. So, it's important to take care of your cables. Most professionals will wrap their cables using the "over/under method." This method uses alternating loops to wrap your cables so they don't get tangled. Start by rolling the first loop clockwise and then roll the next loop counterclockwise. Repeat these steps until the cable is completely rolled up. Avoid tightly rolling your cables because this will strain and damage the cables over time. You can use a twin-bead ponytail holder (I like to call them hairballs), Velcro strap, or even a small piece of rope around your cable to prevent the cable coming loose in storage.

— SEAN'S NOTES —

Having a goal in your recording session is always important. However, I love to grab some objects, head to the Foley Room, and have an exploring session. I enjoy this because it allows me to be creative and not have to stick to a specific plan. It all comes down to what you want to do and make of your recording session.

CHAPTER 6

DIGITAL AUDIO WORKSTATIONS

■ DIGITAL AUDIO WORKSTATIONS

A Digital Audio Workstation (DAW) is the software used for editing sound. DAWs manipulate sound in the same way that Photoshop manipulates pictures. Here's a comparison of their major functions:

DAW	Photoshop
Import	Import
Cut	Crop
Equalize	Color Correction
Process	Filter
Tracks	Layers
Mix	Blend
Export	Export

Since sound is a time-based phenomenon, DAWs use a timeline with the waveform of the audio displayed for the editor to manipulate. You can use a video editor to edit your sound effects, but you will get the best results using software specifically designed for audio.

Here is a breakdown of the basic functions of common DAWs:

- Copy, Cut, Paste
- Splice
- Mix/Cross Fade
- Layer
- Looping
- Pitch Shift
- Mute
- Normalize
- Volume Automation
- Fades
- Recording

■ PLUG-INS

You can do virtually anything with sound in a DAW, especially with the addition of plug-ins. A plug-in is third party software that you add on to your DAW to perform different functions.

The main types of plug-in formats are DirectX, RTAS and VST. Most DAWs will support these and other formats, but you should check the software's system and software requirements before purchasing and installing new plug-ins. Some software and plug-ins require the use of a dongle in order to operate the software. The most popular dongle is a USB key made by PACE called an iLok and is used in an effort to prevent software piracy.

Plug-ins allow audio to pass through different filters and settings that process the sound. Care should be taken when setting the levels of the plug-in to prevent unwanted distortion. You can bypass a plug-in or change the amount of original unprocessed audio heard in the final signal via the dry/wet setting. The dry setting means the sound is heard with zero processing. Increasing this setting toward wet determines how much of the processed sound is heard. A completely wet signal contains only the processed audio.

Here are some common plug-ins used for sound effect creation:

AUTO TRIM/CROP

This tool allows you to make a selection and crop the file around that selection. There are usually parameters that allow you to create micro-fades to prevent clicks and pops at the start and end file.

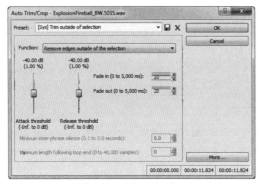

Auto Trim / Crop Plug-In

CHANNEL CONVERTER

This tool allows you to swap channels (e.g., replace the left channel with the right channel and vice versa). You can also convert a mono file into a stereo file by copying and pasting one channel into the other channel. Note, having two channels of audio doesn't necessarily mean that you have a stereo image. If both channels are playing the exact same waveform, the sound will appear mono even though there are two channels.

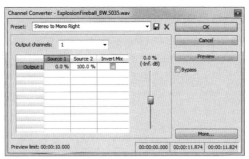

Channel Converter Plug-In

COMPRESSOR

A compressor is a tool that restricts the dynamic range of audio, which allows you to achieve a more consistent and louder volume level. It does this by making the louder parts of your sound quieter and then raising the overall level of the sound. For example, if you have a sound that is pretty quiet except for a few spots that get loud, a compressor will "squash" down the loud parts of the sound and make it sound more even with the softer sections and then raise the volume of the entire sound together. Overusing a compressor can give a pumping effect which distorts your sound, and can even make your sound smaller. The right amount of compression, though, can make your sound fuller and more present.

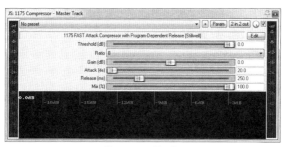

Compressor Plug-In

LIMITER

This tool works like a compressor but with the purpose of preventing a sound from clipping or exceeding a specific volume level.

Limiter Plug-In

EQUALIZER — GRAPHIC

This tool allows you to "color" or "shape" your sound by increasing or decreasing all the frequencies within a specific bandwidth of frequencies. The number of frequency bands depend on the equalizer, with most featuring 5, 10, 20, and 30 bands. Having more frequency bands gives you more precision in adjustments because each bandwidth will be narrower.

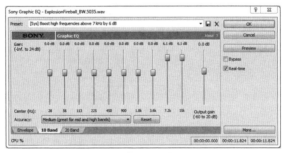

Graphic Equalizer Plug-In

EQUALIZER — PARAGRAPHIC

This tool gives you the highest precision of equalization by using additional controls that allow you to manually adjust the bandwidth of the affected frequencies.

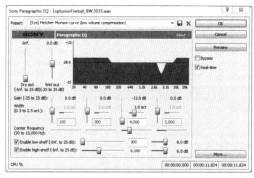

Paragraphic Equalizer Plug-In

DELAY

This tool repeats the sound as many times as you like. This tool repeats the sound as many times as you like. This tool repeats the sound as many times as you like.

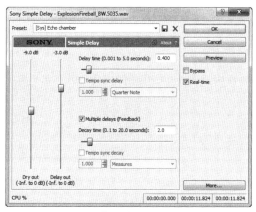

Delay Plug-In

GATE

This tool uses a threshold level to eliminate sound in the file below a specific decibel level. For example, if you have the sound of a clock ticking but there is noise in the background between the ticks at -40db, you can use a gate with a slightly higher threshold to automatically mute sounds below that level. Other controls include attack and release, which determine how fast or slow the gate turns on (attack) or turns off (release).

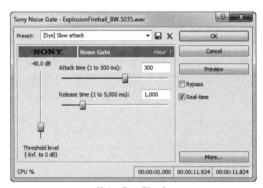

Noise Gate Plug-In

INSERT SILENCE

This tool allows you to insert silence at any point in the audio file. Inserting silence is a powerful tool for timing events in a sound or adding additional time for a plug-in with an effect that exceeds the time in the file such as delay or reverb.

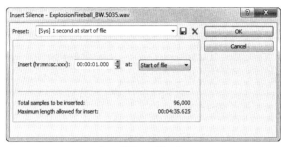

Insert Silence Plug-In

NOISE REDUCTION

This tool allows you to reduce the amount of unwanted noise in a file through various controls or by sampling a section of the noise. Once sampled, the software looks for similar noise in the file and reduces this noise. Advanced noise reduction plug-ins provide Photoshop-style tools to visually remove sound from a graphic display.

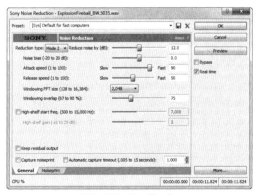

Noise Reduction Plug-In

NORMALIZER

This tool allows you to determine the maximum level of the audio file. The plug-in scans the audio file and raises or lowers the level of the audio file to a specific level value based on either the highest peak in the waveform or the average loudness in the file. Normalizing is a safe-guard against clipping audio in your file.

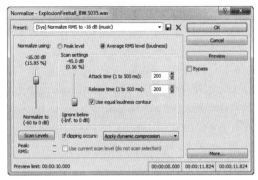

Normalizer Plug-In

PITCH SHIFT

This tool allows the sound to be raised or lowered in pitch. Some pitch shift plug-ins allow you to lower or raise the pitch without changing the duration of the file, whereas others will change the duration of the file to match the new pitch.

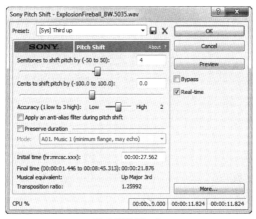

Pitch Shift Plug-In

REVERB

This tool allows the sound to be virtually placed in an environment such as a large hall, church, or sewer. Advanced reverb plug-in IRs (Impulse Responses) can place your sound inside a telephone, metal pipe, or even a vacuum hose for creative effects.

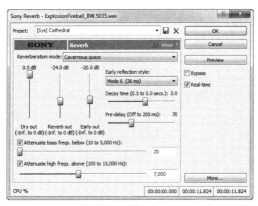

Reverb Plug-In

SPECTRUM ANALYZER

Spectrum analyzers allow you to see all of the frequencies and their relative amplitudes that are present in your audio file in real time. Being able to see this information allows you to see what frequencies make up different sounds. You can also use spectrum analyzers to help train you to recognize different pitches and their corresponding frequencies. There are certain DAWs and audio software that offer a spectrogram view. A spectrogram visualizes the frequencies of your files much like a spectrum analyzer, but has the additional benefit of being able to look at the entire file at once instead of only being able to see the moment-to-moment visual snapshot that a spectrum analyzer allows.

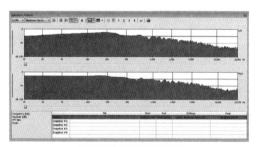

Spectrum Analyzer Plug-In

TIME STRETCH OR TIME COMPRESSION

This tool extends or shortens an audio file without changing the pitch of the sound. This is helpful when you need a sound to fit within a specific length of time. You can create cool digital glitch effects by time-stretching a sound to extreme lengths. Think *The Matrix*.

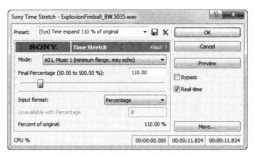

Time Stretch / Compression Plug-In

PLUG-IN CHAINS

You can use plug-ins on your sound one at a time or you can daisy chain them together in a plug-in chain and process the sound all at once. Make sure that you monitor the output level of each plug-in to make sure that your sound doesn't distort. If you experience distortion while using a plug-in chain, the fastest way to solve the problem is to turn off all of the plug-ins in the chain and set the levels of each plug-in individually. Turn on the first plug-in and set your input and output levels. Once you set the level of the first plug-in, move on to the next plug-in and so on.

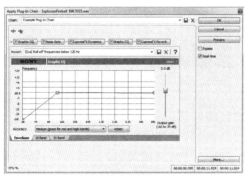

Plug-In Chain

■ MONITORS

Monitors are professional audio speakers designed with a flat frequency response to accurately reproduce the sound. It's important to have a good pair of monitors for editing sound. Some consumer speakers will artificially enhance the sound in an attempt to make it "sound better," but you will get the best results for editing sound by using monitors that have a flat frequency response. If you only have access to lower quality speakers, you can always use your headphones to edit the sound and give the rest of the house some peace and quiet.

Monitors

Caution: Be aware that prolonged exposure to high volumes can cause ear fatigue and ultimately ear damage.

— SEAN'S NOTES —

It is good to know your DAW before jumping into editing your sounds. Growing up, I learned to use a few different DAWs and I found at times that they could get complicated, so I found that it is best to learn the program before editing your prized sounds. If you learn by doing, I recommend that you record a random sound, then import it into your DAW and play around with the different options. This could help you see how each option affects the sound.

CHAPTER 7

EDITING AND DESIGNING SOUND EFFECTS

■ EDITING SOUND

There's a lot of creativity involved with editing. However, there are certain steps that you should take with every file that you edit. To help remember these steps, just L – I – S – T – E – N:

L - Listen Critically
I - Identify Clicks, Pops, and Errors
S - Signal Processing
T - Trim/Crop the File
E - Examine Fades
N - Normalize/Name File

LISTEN CRITICALLY

Carefully listen to the sound effect to determine what you like and what you don't like about the sound. This is the first step in editing sound. Learn to pay attention to every part of the sound in the same way that you would with every element of a picture in Photoshop. If you recorded more than one version of the sound effect, use your favorites and discard the rest. Always start with the best sounds.

IDENTIFY CLICKS, POPS, AND ERRORS

If you hear clicks, pops, or other problems with the sound, then cut them out of the file. Always cut sound on the zero line (the centerline of the waveform on the track) to avoid clicks in your edits. This is easier to do with mono files than with stereo files because it is very rare that both the left and right channels will cross the zero line at the same time. If cutting the errors out of the file creates a click at the edit point, simply cross fade the two sections together. Sometimes a cross fade of a few milliseconds is all it takes to make the edit sound seamless.

SIGNAL PROCESSING

Equalization and compression are used to help polish the sound the way you would use filters in Photoshop to enhance the look of the picture. Remember, using filters is like seasoning food—start with a little and add just enough until it's just the way you like it. You wouldn't dump an entire saltshaker on a basket of fries, so take it easy with the filters.

TRIM/CROP THE FILE

Your sound should start at the beginning of the file. This makes the file easier to use in other projects like videos. If the sound doesn't start at the beginning of the file, then you will have to waste time later trying to find where the sound starts. Some DAWs have a Trim/Crop function that will crop and fade the audio automatically. Make sure you listen to the sound afterwards to verify that nothing was accidentally cut out. It's a good idea to save individual takes as separate files. For example, if you have a file with six car horns, you would save each car horn as a different file.

EXAMINE FADES

The beginning and end of the file should start and end on the zero line. Failure to do so can cause clicks when the file is played in a timeline or in the final project. Most DAWs have an auto-fade feature to prevent these clicks. If not, you will need to manually fade the sound to correct this.

NORMALIZE/NAME FILE

Normalize the audio in the file to make it consistent with other files and easier to use in a project. Quieter sounds like some ambiences may have hiss or other noise that becomes present when the file is normalized.

Peak point normalization anywhere from -18dB to -6dB is acceptable for these types of sounds. Be sure to name the file with a good description that will allow you to identify the sound by the file name without listening to the file.

■ EDITING TIPS

Sound editing is all about making the sound effect the best that it can be. There are no rules for how your sound effect is supposed to sound. So, trust your ears and edit the sound the way you think it should sound. It's all up to you.

Here are some tips on how to edit your sound effects:

NON-DESTRUCTIVE EDITING

Most DAWs manipulate audio files without affecting or destroying the original file. This is called non-destructive editing because the original file is not affected until the file has been saved. However, once the file has been saved or exported, the changes made to the file will be permanent.

ONLY WORK WITH COPIES!

It is important to only work with copies of your files. Never work with the original recordings. If you make a mistake and accidentally delete audio from the original recording, the audio will be lost forever. The very first thing you should do before editing is create a backup copy of your recordings. If possible, these copies should be saved to a separate hard drive or external storage medium. Storing multiple copies of your work in different locations (computer, hard drive, USB stick, network storage, etc.) will ensure that you never lose your recordings.

LEAVE BREADCRUMB TRAILS!

Get in the habit of saving alternate versions of your work. This gives you a breadcrumb trail to follow in case you went down a bunny trail with an idea and ended up somewhere you don't like. This can also happen if you accidentally save the file in a DAW that doesn't allow undos past the save point. Once you get into this habit you will find yourself being bolder in your decisions and taking bigger chances because you know that you have a backup in case you make a mistake. You can also lose your work while editing if your DAW crashes. For this reason, it's important to save your work often. You should also get in the habit of using the save button or the more time-saving CTRL+S/CMD+S shortcuts.

FRANKENSOUND!

Learn to steal pieces and phrases from other parts of the sound to complete holes left from edits or to replace clicks, pops, and other glitches. You can steal the beginning and ending (also called heads and tails, respectively) or sections of other sounds or even copy from within the same file to build your sound effect. For example, let's say that you have three gunshots. The first two have clean trail-offs (when the bullet continues to travel through the air after the initial blast), but the third has a blemish (bird chirps, bullet shell lands on the ground, or even the reloading of the weapon by an overzealous shooter). You can steal the trail-off from one of the first two files and replace the trail-off in the third file from the borrowed trail-off.

Editing is about deciding which parts of the sound you want to keep and discarding the rest. It doesn't matter *how you make the sound effect*. It only matters *how the sound effect sounds*. Using the Frankensound technique will allow you to meticulously construct the perfect sound effect.

BALANCE THE STEREO FIELD

Ambiences, drones, and other consistent stereo sound effects should have a balanced stereo field. While it's okay if random sounds occur in only one channel, if the left channel is consistently louder than the right channel or vice versa, the sound will appear lopsided to the listener. Adjust the volumes of the channels to balance out the stereo field. You can use volume automation for sounds that have only a section of the file that is unbalanced. For recordings that are off-balanced but can still be used as mono sounds (e.g., a door closing), copy the channel with the best sound to both channels. In general, it's best to not pan your sound effects when editing. Once you save a pan in a file it will always be panned. Instead, you should keep the sound centered/balanced and make the panning decisions when using the sound effect in a project non-destructively.

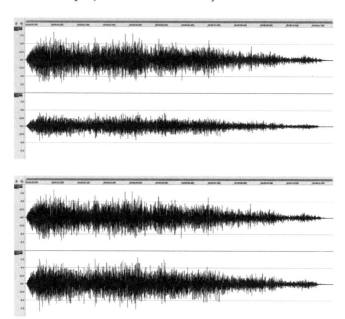

Top: Unbalanced Stereo File, Bottom: Balanced Stereo File

THE DOPPLER EFFECT!

The changes in the pitch of a sound as it approaches and passes is known as the Doppler effect. The phenomenon is named after its discoverer, Austrian physicist Christian Doppler, and is the result of higher frequencies building up from an approaching object and then transitioning to lower frequencies as the object passes. You can see this effect at work in a simple experiment in a pool or lake. With your hand partially submerged in water, move your hand in one direction. As your hand moves through the water, the water is pushed forward resulting in high frequency waves. However, low frequency waves follow behind the hand. This explains how sound waves change pitch when you hear a car horn as it passes by.

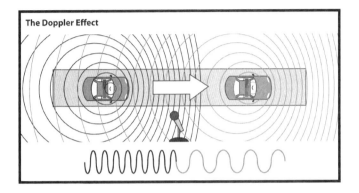

The Doppler Effect

Editing sounds with the Doppler effect can be challenging because the changes in pitch will be noticeable if you remove a section of the sound. This will result in a jump in pitch during an edit or give a warbling effect during a cross fade. It takes a little bit of effort, but with some patience, you can often find a suitable point and duration to cross fade an edit point with the Doppler effect. The goal of the cross fade is to make the transition appear as one seamless take.

COLORING YOUR SOUND!

Equalization, often called EQ, is the process of balancing the frequencies of a sound. This is like color correction for a picture, but instead of working with light waves you are working with sound waves. Sometimes equalization is used to correct problems with the sound. For example, you can use an equalizer to remove low rumble sounds in a recording by selecting and reducing those frequencies from the sound. Other times, equalization is used to enhance a sound by exaggerating different frequencies to make the sound brighter (high frequencies), harsher (mid frequencies) or muddier (low frequencies). In general, you should use equalization sparingly, but don't be afraid to experiment.

■ SOUND EFFECTS FILE NAMES

When you save your audio file, you will need to give the file a name. Be descriptive with the name of the file so that you can easily locate the sound later. It's important to keep your naming structure consistent. Here's an example of a common naming system used by professional sound effects libraries:

1. Category
2. Noun
3. Verb
4. Description
5. Number

For example, if you use the naming structure above for the sound effect of a zombie moaning the word "brains," the file name would look like this:

Horror Zombie Moan Brains 01

Here's a breakdown of the naming system:

CATEGORY

Placing the category at the beginning of the file name will allow you to quickly organize and search for files. This allows files in the same category to be grouped together in folders and searches. Here are some examples of sound effects categories:

- Ambience
- Animals
- Cartoon
- Emergency
- Explosions
- Fire
- Foley
- Food
- Footsteps
- Horror
- Household
- Humans
- Impacts
- Industry
- Music
- Office
- Production Elements
- Science Fiction
- Sports
- Technology
- Vehicles (Planes, Trains, Automobiles, and Boats)
- Water

- Weapons
- Weather

Since zombies are horrible creatures, we would use "Horror" for the category.

NOUN

The noun is a word or simple word phrase for the object creating the sound. In the example above, the zombie is the object creating the sound.

VERB

The action of the sound is typically used in simple present tense form. For example, the word "moan" is used instead of "moaning."

DESCRIPTION

The description of the sound allows you to add more detail to the name to help distinguish the sound from other files with a similar Category, Noun, Verb structure. So, the word "brains" is added to indicate the zombie is moaning the word.

NUMBER

Computer operating systems will require you to give each file a unique name. For this reason, files that require the same name are given a number at the end of the file. In the example above, the number is zero-filled. This means that all numbers are expressed as double digits. Therefore, numbers 1-9 will have a zero in front to fill in space as a digit. This is helpful for keeping your files in numeric order for software and operating systems that would otherwise place the files out of numerical order.

For example: 1, 10, 11, 12, 13, 14, 15, 16, 17, 18, 19, 2, 20, 21, 22, etc.

Zero-filling numbers will compensate for this and keep the files in numerical order.

For example: 01, 02, 03, 04, 05, 06, 07, 08, 09, 10, 11, 12, etc.

While you may only have one version of a sound right now, you may record other versions in the future. Using the zero-fill technique will prevent you from renaming files to account for the new additions. For example, I recorded over 1,000 sound effects my first year of recording!

■ METADATA

Metadata is the information stored within the file to be used by software during searches. SoundMiner is the professional software program used by most audio professionals, but iTunes can be a low-cost alternative for beginners. The use of metadata allows for more descriptive words and helpful information to be included in the file since operating systems have a limit on the character count for a file name.

— SEAN'S NOTES —

In my opinion, editing your sound is just as important as recording it. I love being creative and designing things so this is right up my alley and hopefully yours too. But also remember to stay organized as well. I have a small case of OCD, so I feel that it is imperative to keep your edited sounds organized and easily accessible using the naming method suggested earlier. Just remember to be creative and have fun when editing your sounds.

CHAPTER 8

SOUND DESIGN TRICKS

Sound design is the process of manipulating audio to create a specific sound, emotion, or environment. In the professional sound industry, sound designers are in charge of molding and shaping not only the individual sounds, but also the soundscape or soundtrack of the story. The process of sound design takes sound editing to a whole new level.

The goal of designing sound effects is to create a sound so convincing that the listener will think it is the real thing.

Here are some common and advanced sound design tricks:

AUTOMATION
DAWs allow you to automate certain functions like volume, pan, mute, and even plug-in parameters. The

automation requires key frames or anchor points to indicate where on the timeline the automation should take place. Using automation gives you extreme precision when panning a sound from left to right, or raising/lowering the volume of the track.

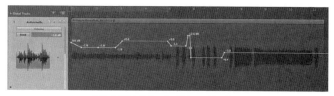

Automation Using the Volume Envelope

PITCH SHIFTING

One of the most commonly used tricks in sound design is pitch shifting. With pitch shifting, you can make a sound larger or smaller, make a sound speed up or slow down and even lower the pitch so low that the original sound is completely unrecognizable. You can even pitch a sound up or down, process the sound with an effect like reverb, then pitch the sound back to the original pitch.

LOOPING

Looping is an extremely useful technique for ambiences, creating machines and motors, extending the length of a small sample by playing it repeatedly, and tons of other creative sounds like drones and science fiction sound effects like force fields. To loop a sound, simply copy the section you would like to repeat and paste as many cop-ies of that sound as you would like. For example, if you have a three-minute scene that takes place in a park, but your ambience sound is only one minute, you can loop the sound two more times to fill the scene. If the loop point is noticeable because the background changes, you can cross-fade the loop point. Longer cross-fades can make the loop point vanish, giving the illusion that the sound simply continues.

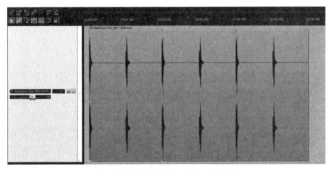

Looping the Tick of an Alarm Clock

Mono sounds are easier to loop than stereo sounds because there are few chances of both waveforms cross-ing the zero line at the same time. Equalizing low frequencies below 80Hz can make the waveform easier to manage by offering more frequent crossings at the zero line. This will eliminate clicks and pops that can occur at the loop point. If you're not sure if there are any clicks or if the loop point is noticeable, close your eyes while you listen.

For sounds with a rhythmic pattern like a machine or ticking clock, you will need to be more precise with your loop point to match the timing. You can also insert silence between the loops for mechanical sounds with rhythm or timing like clock ticks. Organic sounds can sound artificial if they are too precise. For example, if you loop birds chirping in the background of a park ambience exactly five seconds apart, you might notice the pattern. To break up the pattern, stagger the loop pattern by varying the timing between the loops. There is no right method, so tweak the sound until it feels right. Warning— the looping technique can be addictive!

REVERSING

Sounds played backwards can create cool effects. This is a useful trick for suction sounds, creepy drones, and even looping sounds together. Reversing a sound, applying an effect, and then reversing the sound again can create otherworldly sound effects.

VOCALIZING

Sometime you can use your own voice as the source. This is about as old school as it gets. Everyone loves to make sound effects with their mouths when telling a story. So, why not experiment with your voice and see what cool sounds you can make? You can even layer your voice sounds underneath other sounds. In fact, Ben Burtt used this technique for parts of R2-D2's voice.

LAYERING

You can use the tracks in your DAW to layer multiple sounds together. This technique adds infinite possibilities to what you can create. You can layer multiple ambiences together to create the perfect background, combine multiple copies of a small group of people talking to make them sound like a larger group, and even build complex scenes like a battlefield with gunshots and explosions.

OFFSET LAYERING

Offset layering can allow you to make a boring sound more active by combining different sections of the recording together. For example, if you have a six-minute recording of a grocery store with only a few people in it, you can cut the sound into three different two-minute sections and layer them together to make the grocery store sound like there are more customers. This technique can be used to make creeks sound like giant rivers and make your shower sound like a waterfall.

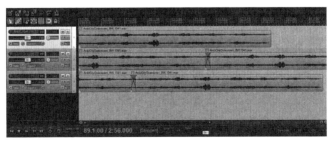

Offset Layering the Ambience of a City

PITCH LAYERING

You can copy the same sound to multiple tracks and change each track to a different pitch. The pitch layering technique can be used to suggest movement like an object pass-by going from a higher pitch to a lower pitch and can make sounds fuller, brighter, and deeper. You can use the entire track or only use a portion of the track mixed in with the other tracks.

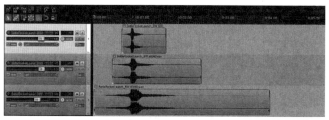

Pitch Layering a Bottle Rocket

MIXING

Audio tracks are combined together in a process called mixing. How the tracks are blended and balanced together will make a huge difference in your sound. If you have lots of tracks playing at the same level in relation to each other, the sound becomes muddy and hard to understand. While it might be tempting to make everything loud, you'll want to exercise a little restraint here. Think less is more and build from there.

Focus on which sound or track is important at each moment and adjust the levels so that the important parts are heard. Make sure that changes in level don't stick out and feel unnatural. Use smooth fades when possible. Some tracks may need additional equalization to help blend in well with the other tracks. Finally, make sure that your level does not clip.

It doesn't matter how you make the sound. Just make the sound cool!

— SEAN'S NOTES —

I found that these sound design tricks are good to have up your sleeve. For example, a few years back, I designed an office ambience. When doing this, I used a number of these design tricks. First, I looped a track of a crowd and set that as the background. Then I layered office sound effects such as telephone rings and copy machines to add to the looped background sound. The offset layering trick also came in handy so I could have the office sounds occur at different times. Through that process, I found that these tricks definitely do come in handy.

CHAPTER 9

100 SOUND EFFECTS TO MAKE AT HOME

Now that we've discussed sound effects, the recording gear, techniques, editing, and sound design, let's start making some noise! Here's a list of sound effects you can record using common things around the house as well as some uncommon ways to use them:

ACID

To create the sound of bubbling acid, pour a small amount of water onto a hot pan. Keep the microphone low and to the side of the pan so that the steam doesn't affect the recording or damage your microphone.

AIR CANS

Air cans, often called air dusters, are great for science fiction airbursts. Get creative about spraying the air through different objects like pipes and tubes to see what sounds you can come up with. Keep in mind; you should never spray the microphone directly with air because it can cause permanent damage to the microphone.

ALARM CLOCKS

I know they are annoying and you hate hearing that awful sound, but alarm clocks are useful sound effects. With some pitching and processing, digital alarm clocks can also be used for spaceship alarms and buzzers, whereas the antique bell alarm clocks can be used for school bells and fire alarms. Don't forget to record the buttons and the sound of the clock being wound.

ALIEN VOICES

Aliens do exist! At least, that's what your friends will think when they hear the alien voices you record. Cool alien voices, like some of the iconic ones in *Star Wars*, are often created by processing an actor's voice to make it sound out-of-this-world. The most typical effects used in processing alien voices are pitching, chorus, and harmonizers, but feel free to try something completely different! Be creative with the language that the alien speaks and include vocal inflections and emotion in the voice to make it sound believable. Of course, you don't have to use your voice at all. Some of the alien voices in *Star Wars* like Chewbacca's were created using sound clips from different animals. Try to record an alien language using only tongue clicks in your mouth. You are limited only by your imagination.

APPLAUSE

You don't need to have a stadium of 10,000 clapping fans to create the sound of one! You can clap your hands all by yourself and layer the recording as many times as you'd like to create the perfect applause. You can use whichever reverb setting you'd like to create the right environment for the hand claps. Keep in mind, the longer you clap your hands, the more realistic the sound will be when you layer and loop the recordings. Shorter takes will have a noticeable loop point and tend to sound cartoonish or fake.

APPLIANCES

Home appliances like vacuum cleaners, washers, and dryers can be great sources for science fiction sounds when pitched up or down, looped, layered, etc. Dryer doors can be used for rocket ship doors or sources for explosions when pitched down really low. Some dryers have a buzzer that goes off when the load is finished that can be used for things like game show buzzers or slowed down and looped for science fiction alarms. Experiment and see what you can come up with.

ATTIC TREASURES

Everyone usually has at least one parent that's a hoarder. Find their stash of treasures from yesteryear and record the sounds. Check the attic, basement, garage, and anywhere you might find old unused stuff like typewriters, rotary phones, phonographs, VHS players, CD Players. Note, when working with tape-based electronics like tape recorders and VHS players, never use personal tapes to work with to prevent accidentally erasing or otherwise damaging things like family home movies. Instead, find an unused blank tape or something with no sentimental value. Keep in mind, if your parent is a little reluctant on letting you go through their stuff, be sure to treat everything with care and put it back exactly how you found it. This way, they'll be more likely to let you record other things in the future.

BALLOONS

You can create interesting sounds with balloons. They can be stretched, blown up, deflated, filled with water, and dropped for splats. You can squeeze the end of the balloon as air is being released to make the sounds of insects like mosquitoes. Popping a balloon can be used for an indoor gunshot.

BATHTUB

Bathtubs are a great source for bubbles and splashes. Recording water drips in a bathtub and adding a reverb plug-in in your DAW can create realistic cave sounds. The higher the water drip, the deeper the sound. You can change the type of environment for the water drips by changing the reverb settings. For example, the same water drips can be made to sound like they are coming from inside a sewer just by using a plug-in. Also, try experimenting with different water levels for different types of sounds. And don't forget to record single drips. Remember, water and electronics do not play well together, so be sure to keep your gear dry!

BED CREAKS

Wood frame beds can cause all kinds of cool creaks that can be used for pirate ships and other wood structures including an angry haunted house. The trick is to find exactly where the creaks are coming from and how to reproduce the creak. Make sure that you are recording before you start making creaks because some objects will stop making the creaking sound if you wear out the friction point.

BEEPS

Most DAWs will allow you to create beeps through a tone generator, but if you don't have one, smoke detectors, toys, cameras, microwaves, and other digital appliances are great sources for recording beeps. There are also tons of free tone generators on the app stores.

BODY FALLS

In the movie business, body falls are typically recorded by dropping leather coats on various surfaces. You can stuff the coat with books or other items to make the sound heavier. You can also swing the coat into the surface for faster and harder impacts. Recording multiple takes of the body fall allows you to edit the best parts together for the perfect fall.

BOILING WATER

Recording boiling water can be dangerous, so be sure to have permission to use the stove and keep your hands and the gear away from the steam. Place the recorder to the side of the pot and angle the microphone down toward the water. Never place the microphone directly over boiling water as the steam can damage the microphone. You can simulate the sound of boiling water by blowing through a straw into water. Layering multiple takes together will give you a more realistic sound.

Recording Water Boiling

BUBBLE WRAP

Bubble wrap is on the list because, let's face it, everyone loves to pop bubble wrap. Now you have a reason to pop more bubble wrap!

BUBBLES

Bubbles are created by blowing through a straw or hose into a container with water. Four things determine the sound of the bubbles:

1. The size of the tube you blow through.
2. The force of air blown through the tube.
3. The size of the container of water.
4. The depth of the tube in the water.

BUTTONS/SWITCHES

You'd be surprised how many buttons and switches are in your house. Every room has a light switch. Electronics have buttons. Appliances, gadgets, and even lawnmowers all have buttons and switches. Spend a day going around the house to see how many you can record.

CARS

You can record tons of stuff from a car without even turning the engine on. There's the hood, doors, and trunk opening and closing, switches and dials on the dashboard and steering column, servomotors from the powered seats, windows rolling up and down, blinkers, etc. The stuff you record in a car can be used for all kinds of sounds. For example, the powered seat servomotors can be excellent sources for science fiction gears, the windows can be used for spaceship doors, and the switches can be used for buttons on a control panel.

For quieter sounds, you're better off recording inside the garage to shield the recording from neighborhood sounds. However, if you slam a door inside a garage, it will sound like a car door closing inside of a garage. This is because of the reverb from the walls. The solution is to record these types of sounds outside of the garage.

Even if there is some background noise from the neighborhood, you can edit the sound before the action and edit/fade the unwanted sounds after the door is closed. This will leave you with a perfectly clean recording of a car door closing. Be sure to turn your headphones off before recording the car horn. The horn is already loud to the human ear, so you don't want to amplify that sound in your ears.

Now it's time to record the engine. Where you place the microphone around the car will determine the type of sound you will hear. The most common places to record a car's engine are the engine compartment through the grill, the tailpipe, and inside the car for an interior perspective. The grill perspective gives a brighter sound with more focus on the moving parts of the engine, whereas the tailpipe perspective gives you more of a deep, throatier purr to the engine. Note that the tailpipe is producing exhaust fumes from the engine so be sure to protect the microphone by positioning it perpendicular to the pipe to avoid wind noise. The interior perspective works great for backgrounds in scenes where the actors are driving in a car.

CARTOON PUNCH/SLAP

The traditional cartoon punch or slap can be super easy to create. All you need is a single rubber latex glove. Stretch the glove like a rubber band and let it go for the perfect snap. This can also be done with large balloons, but latex gloves tend to sound better.

CENSOR BLEEP

A censor bleep can make it sound like someone used a bad word even if the word said wasn't really a bad word. The censor bleeps used in broadcast television are typically 1kHz tones. You can use a simple tone generator app or a plug-in in your DAW to dial in the correct frequency. Create a long sample so that you can extend the bleep if the person on screen goes on an explicit tirade.

CLOCKS

The ticks and tocks of clocks are pretty iconic and help sell the concept of time to your audience. However, clocks are really, really quiet. A good trick to record a clock ticking is to get the microphone really close. Background may be an issue, but don't worry. When you edit the recording, you only need one "tic" and one "tock." So, you can mute the background noise between the tic and tock leaving you with a clean sound. Once you've edited the sound, you can copy/paste the two tics and loop the sound for as long as you want. Additionally, if you only have one tic, you can pitch a copy of the tic lower to make it a tock.

CLOTH TEARS

Old t-shirts and bed sheets can be used for cloth tears. You can start the tear with a pair of scissors. Make the first tear in the center for heavier sounds and continue tearing each subsequent section in half. For thinner and higher-pitched tears, make the strips narrower.

COMPUTERS

Record the sound of your laptop or desktop computer booting up and don't forget to record typing on the keyboard. Avoid randomly pressing the keys for typing sequences, as it doesn't sound convincing. Instead, try typing actual words and phrases, as the pacing of the keys will sound more realistic. Also, be sure to include single key presses of the space bar, enter key, and letter keys, which will each sound different. Note that the computer should be turned off while recording the keyboard to eliminate the sound of the computer's fan. Finally, record peripherals like printers, scanners, and mouse clicks.

CRASHES

Crash sounds make the action come to life on the screen. Most of the time, the props used in movies to visually create a cool crash aren't dangerous at all. In video games, the crashes aren't even real, they're simply ones and zeros projected on the screen. So, it's up to you to create the sound of the chaos and debris.

Recording a Television Set being smashed with a Sledgehammer!

A good sound effects recordist loves to raid the garbage, preferably before something is thrown away. Because if it's going to get trashed anyway, why not record it getting smashed first! Be sure to check out the sonic treasures your neighbors are pitching to the curb each week. You might get lucky and find some goodies to record destroying. If you've got an appetite for destruction, then never underestimate the power of garbage day. Always be careful when rummaging through the garbage, as there can often be dangerous things like broken glass or light bulbs that have been thrown away.

When recording crashes, be sure to wear:

1. Safety Glasses
2. Gloves
3. Earplugs

Be aware of flying debris when smashing things. If you are breaking glass, be sure to protect yourself and your equipment from glass shards. For loud crashes, be sure to wear earplugs!

DOORBELLS

The problem with recording doorbells is that the doorbell is located inside the house, but the button to ring it is outside. The catch is, if you leave the front door open you run the risk of hearing traffic or ambience from the neighborhood during your doorbell recording. If possible, have someone stand outside and operate the button for you while you record the doorbell inside. Be sure to record single rings as well as impatient rings. Remember, your neighbors will have different doorbells than you do so ask if you can record theirs as well.

DOORS

Different types of doors will have different types of sounds, and there are a lot of different types of doors. For example, doors can be metal, aluminum, solid wood, hollow wood, glass, or even a combination of the above. While it might not be necessary to record every door in your house, it's a great idea to record every type of door in your house.

A door knock will sound different through the door, so it can be helpful to have someone do the knocking for you. If you are recording alone, you can still knock on the door from the same side you are recording on. You can leave the recorder on one side and knock on the other, but be sure to check your levels and listen back to the recording to make sure it sounds good.

Door opens are more of a challenge than door closes because they are usually limited to a creaking sound as the hinges swing open. If the hinges do not squeak (which happens a lot), then you really can't hear the door open. Don't worry. You can always create a creaking sound from other sources including another door. Be mindful of air movement created by the door when recording the sound of the door opening and closing. Use a windscreen if necessary.

DRAWERS

For drawers, try to position the microphone underneath or to the side of the drawer. This is usually where

the source sound is created. Record the drawers opening and closing at different speeds and intensities. You
can also perform objects being placed in the drawer
and removed.

DUCT TAPE

Every household has a roll of duct tape. Record ripping
the tape of the roll, tearing strips and even rolling the
roll of duct tape across different surfaces.

EATING

The next time you bite into a big juicy apple, make sure
you record the chomp. When recording eating sounds,
try to record with your mouth open for clearer sounds.
Closing your mouth will muffle the sound. If you need
the sound of chewing with the mouth closed, try using
crunchier food like crackers, nachos, or peanuts to make
the chewing more noticeable.

EGG TIMERS

Egg timers can be used for clock ticks or a ticking bomb.
Some timers have a bell that gives a single ding. Try to
record just the ding without the ticking of the timer.
You can pitch the bell way down to create the sound
of a giant church bell. Other timers will have a ringing bell. These rings can be used to simulate an old
telephone ring.

ELECTRONICS

You can record video game consoles and Blu-ray player
servomotors when a disc is inserted or ejected. The

servomotors can be used as science fiction doors or lay-ered and combined to create robot movements.

EXERCISE EQUIPMENT

There's a good chance that there is some exercise equip-ment gathering dust somewhere in your house. Whether it's a weight bench, treadmill, or exercise bike, see what sounds you can record. Free weights are great sources for manholes and clunky metal sounds, especially when pitched down.

FANS

The very nature of a fan is to move air. Obviously, this creates a problem for recording the fan head-on. Recording behind or to the side of the fan can solve this problem. For ceiling fans, you can usually place the microphone underneath the center of the fan. Be careful not to get too close!

FLAG

Shaking and moving a pillowcase back and forth can create the sound of a flag flapping in the wind. The tim-ing and pacing of the flaps should be random like the wind, so avoid steady rhythms and repeating patterns. Sails can be created using the same technique with bed sheets.

FIRE

Backyard fire pits, fireplaces, BBQ grills, metal trash cans and empty oil drums are safe ways of recording fires with a parent's permission. If your fire sounds quiet and weak, record longer takes so you can layer them for bigger fires. When recording fire, make sure that the microphone is a safe distance from the heat or the microphone's diaphragm could melt or become damaged. Keep the microphone lower to the ground and to the side of the fire. If you can't record real fire, you can create the sound of fire by crinkling plastic sheets of cellophane.

Recording a Bonfire

FIREWORKS

Legal fireworks that are commonly used in driveways during holidays are great sources for explosions, gunshots, and magic. Care should be taken to ensure that your microphone and yourself are at a safe distance. If you are using an external microphone, use a cable long enough to position yourself at a safe distance from the fireworks. If you are using a handheld recorder, you should position the recorder at a safe distance from the fireworks, press record and move to a safer distance after testing your recording levels.

Recording Fireworks with the crew from the Detroit Chop Shop

FOOD

The good news about being a sound effects recordist is that you get to play with your food. Food is a common prop used for sound effects. The sound of the snakes moving beneath Indiana Jones' feet in the movie *Raiders of the Lost Ark* was made by running fingers through a casserole. In the same film, snake hisses were created by ripping long strips off masking tape from a pane of glass. Pretty harmless sources for venomous snakes! You can make interesting sounds with peanut shells, dry pasta, dog food, nachos, crackers, wet macaroni, etc. Of course, there's always fruit and vegetables, but they're so much fun we're going to give them their own section.

Casserole! Why did it have to be casserole! *Raiders of the Lost Ark,*
©1981 Luscasfilm Ltd., All Rights Reserved.

FOOTSTEPS

Footsteps are the results of two objects: the footwear and the surface that you're walking on. Professional sound studios in Hollywood have rooms with various surfaces on the floor specifically for recording footsteps. Many Foley artists will have a collection of shoes, each with a different and unique sound. Some Foley artists will use their hands to perform the action instead of their feet if the shoes they like don't fit their hands.

The traditional method for recording footsteps is called the heel-to-toe method. This means that the heel of the foot touches the ground first followed by the ball of the foot and toes. If you are adding footsteps to a video that you are editing you will need to watch the footage to find the precise frame when the foot touches the ground to add the sound effect. If you cannot see the foot because of the camera angle, simply watch for the shoulder of the actor to dip to the lowest point during motion. This will indicate when their foot has touched the ground.

A good editing tip is to pay attention to the sound of the footsteps that you are using. Ask yourself these questions: Does this sound like the shoe I see on the screen? Does the sound match the surface that the actor is walking on? Does the pace of the footsteps match the action in the video? Finally, listen closely and ask yourself if the footsteps sound too loud or soft. The goal is for the audience to not realize that you added the sound effects, so be sneaky.

Think of all the surfaces that you might have in your home to walk on. These different surfaces might include hardwood floors, tile, marble, carpet, as well as cement floors in the garage or basement. Outside the house you might have grass, rocks, dirt, gravel, sand or landscaping such as woodchips. Try recording footsteps on as many surfaces as you can find at home. Remember to record as many things as possible with each pair of shoes— walking, running, stomping, jumping, scuffs, slides, and anything else you can think of.

FRUITS AND VEGETABLES

Believe it or not, the sound of the zombie apocalypse comes from your grocery store! Fruits and veggies are on the menu for things to record when it comes to wet, juicy, slimy, and disgusting sounds. Recording the sounds is actually the easy part. Cleaning up the mess is where the real work comes in. Protect your microphone and recording gear from the splashes that will undoubtedly occur. For protection, try to use towels instead of plastic because the plastic can be heard in the recording when hit by debris.

GARAGE DOOR

You can record an automatic garage door by pointing the microphone at the opener or at the wheels inside the track. You can follow the wheels with the recorder or stand stationary and record the wheels moving past the microphone. Placing microphones at both the opener and on the wheels and recording them to separate channels will allow you to mix the sounds together later. If you have an automatic garage door, ask for permission to disconnect the door from the opener to allow you to manually control the door opening and closing.

GARDEN HOSE

A garden hose offers an unending supply of water that can be used for things like rain, fountains, and waterfalls. The surface you perform on as well as the pressure of the stream of water will make the biggest effect on your sound. Layering multiple takes together can create some pretty amazing sound effects, but be sure to keep your gear dry.

GARDENING TOOLS

If you get stuck doing lawn chores over the weekend, turn the afternoon into a recording session. You can record yourself raking leaves, trimming shrubs, shoveling landscaping materials, and even mowing the lawn. But try not to smile while you are recording because your parents may think you enjoy chores and give you more to do.

GHOSTS

Creating voices from beyond the grave doesn't require a Ouija board—just a microphone. Record your best ghost impression and then reverse the sound in your DAW. Then, add some reverb with a tail of a few seconds. After that, reverse the sound again and listen to the results. You can use other effects like chorus, delay, and pitch to create spooky visitors from another dimension.

GLASS SQUEAKS

Glass surfaces make really cool squeaks when wet. If you have a glass shower door, you can move a dry hand down the surface. Try varying the speed that you move your hand. Experiment by pitching, layering, and cross-fading multiple takes together in your DAW to see what cool things you can create.

GRASS

You can record grass outside, but since grass is pretty quiet and the outdoors is pretty noisy, it's a good idea to record the grass indoors. A common Foley trick for grass is using piles of tape from audio cassettes or VHS tapes. Be sure to check with your parents before you destroy their favorite KISS cassettes!

GUILLOTINE

Combining several common household items can easily make the gruesome sound of a guillotine decapitating its victim. The sound consists of a blade sliding down and chopping off a head. For the blade sliding down, you can scrape steak knives or larger cooking knives together combined with a wood drawer being pushed in or out. For the head chop, you can drop a watermelon for the juicy impact combined with a head of lettuce for the sound of the head falling to the ground.

GUNSHOTS

Gunshots are typically recorded on gun ranges and in the desert. This is not only done for safety reasons, but for sonic reasons as well. Gunshots are essentially very short but very loud cracks. If you can't get permission or access to a gun range, gunshots can be simulated by slamming doors or lighting off firecrackers and then combining them with fast impact sounds like dropping a metal box or slamming metal trash can lids together. You can layer the recordings and use EQ and pitch shift to beef up the sound.

Recording an authentic M1 Carbine from World War II

Machine gun sounds can be made during editing by looping a single gunshot, but it tends to sound very cartoony. You'll make more realistic machine gun sounds by editing multiple recordings together. Keep in mind when recording, whatever source you use for a gunshot will probably be loud, so don't forget to wear earplugs!

HAIR PULLS

You don't have to pull your hair out to try to figure out how to make the sound of pulling your hair out. Ripping old bed sheets, separating long Velcro strips, and tearing pieces of carpet can make for a convincing solution. And best of all, no one loses their hair.

HEARTBEAT

You don't need a doctor or even a stethoscope to record a convincing heartbeat. You can tap your hand or smack a couch, pound on your bare chest or even punch a leather coat for the heartbeat sound. Pacing is important, but you can always edit the sound for the correct speed later. Plus, you will probably need to pitch the sound down, which will affect the pacing of the heartbeat. If the sound is too bright, equalize the sound in your DAW by reducing high and upper-mid frequencies. You can also add some low frequencies to give it a nice thump.

HORSE HOOVES

Using coconut shells for horses galloping is one of the oldest tricks in the movie business. To start, cut a coconut in half and clean out both halves of the shell. Next, find a good surface like dirt or grass and perform the hoofbeats by holding the back of the shells in each hand with the open half facing downward. Practice the pacing of the steps to mimic the rhythm of the horse's steps.

HOT WATER BOTTLES

An old Hollywood sound effect trick is to create tire screeches by rubbing a hot water bottle filled with air against a smooth surface like a table. The friction against the rubber sounds just like a sharp turn during a high-speed car chase in a movie. Pitching the sound down can make it sound more realistic, but you can usually get good screeches without processing the sound at all.

HUMAN SOUNDS

Recording human sounds is probably the easiest thing to record because you have a recorder and you are a human. The job is half done! The only thing left to find is a quiet place to record.

Here are some ideas for human sounds to record: sneezing, snoring, burping, farting, coughing, sniffing, screaming, crying, vomiting, sighing, breathing, gasping, gulping, spitting, kissing, grunting, laughing, whistling, yawning, and slurping. Don't forget to try animal sounds with your voice. See what your recordings sound like when you pitch them up and down.

ICE

Freezing a wet towel in the freezer and slowly opening the towel in front of the microphone can create the sound of ice cracking. You can also use ice trays for ice cracks or freeze cooking pans with a shallow layer of water. If you live in a colder climate, you can freeze water overnight by leaving containers filled with water outside. Avoid recording ice on lakes or ponds because this is a potential risk for the gear and an obvious safety hazard for you. If you do record a frozen lake, be sure to stay on the shore and record the edges of the ice.

INSECTS

Insects aren't really keen on doing what they're told to do, so it can be difficult to work with them. Plus, they can be hard to locate. But sometimes you get lucky. I'll never forget recording a fly in my studio. My assistant noticed that there was a fly in the recording booth, so we decided to set up a couple of microphones. We left the room for a couple of hours with the recorder rolling. This allowed the room to stay perfectly quiet so the microphones would only hear the sound of the fly's wings. When we listened to the recording, we were amazed to find dozens of pass bys from the fly with its wings buzzing closely past the microphones. The fly even landed on the microphone. We layered the sounds on top of each other and created really cool beehives and swarms of flies. So before you shoo a fly out of your room, be sure to record it first!

Crickets are pretty common insects and not too difficult to find. However, you can always go to the pet store and purchase insects as they are commonly sold as food for other animals. I have a friend who does amazing cricket sounds with his mouth. Sometimes, he sounds better than the real thing. If you can't record the real thing, you can make homemade insect chirps by recording your voice and pitching the sound up—a lot! Try giggling, laughing, and screaming or just make weird sounds with your mouth.

If you need the sound of bugs moving around, you'll need to get a little creative because bugs have really tiny feet, so the microphone won't be able to hear their footsteps loud enough to record them. Then again, if the bug is big enough to hear their footsteps, you probably don't want to get close enough to record them. The solution for making insect footsteps is to perform the footsteps with your fingers. Use plastic ink pen caps or paperclips taped to your fingers to sound like their feet.

Recording Insect Footsteps with Pen Caps

You can put some leaves, sand, dirt, or even tree bark in a plastic bin and record indoors because the sounds will be soft and you will need a quiet environment to record. If you can hear the plastic sound of the bin, try placing a towel inside it before you add your dirt or whatever surface you're trying to replicate. Experiment with different speeds and surfaces or even try using all your fingers from both your hands. Be sure to remove any jewelry like rings or bracelets before performing so they don't make any unwanted sounds during your recording.

When you listen back to your recording in your DAW, try playing the sound back at faster and slower speeds by varying the pitch. Speeding up the sound will make the insect run faster than your fingers can move. Keep in mind, when you pitch the sound up, the duration of the recording will become much shorter. So, if you want three seconds of an insect walking, you might want to record ten seconds or more.

IRONING BOARD

Ironing boards offer a great variety of metal screeches and squeaks that can be fun to design cool sounds with. Slowing the recordings down can create the effect of being inside a submarine when you add a convincing reverb effect to the recording. You can also make the sound of a scary spaceship or a large metal structure like an abandoned bridge. Experiment and see what you can come up with.

KITCHEN APPLIANCES

The kitchen can offer an entire day's worth of recording between the dishwasher, refrigerator, oven, stove, microwave, blender, garbage disposal, and other time-saving tools that make noise. Most kitchens aren't very quiet and the room often has some reverb. If possible, get permission to take some of the smaller appliances to a quieter location. For large appliances, pick a time to record when there's not a lot of activity in the house to make sure you get the quietest recordings. Since you're in the kitchen, don't forget to record the silverware, plates, pots, and pans.

LAWN SPRINKLERS

The trick to recording lawn sprinklers is to do so without getting the recorder wet! Thankfully, the source of the sound is at the head of the sprinkler where the water comes out. By standing on the opposite side of the water you can safely place the recorder close to the sound source without getting the gear wet.

LAWNMOWER

Lawnmowers are inherently loud, so you will need to stand a few feet away and watch the levels on your recorder to make sure that you don't clip. Beware of flying debris from underneath the lawnmower. Also, never flip a lawnmower upside down while it is running! You can safely record the sound while it is in the normal upright position. While you're in the garage, be sure to record the hedge trimmers, weed trimmers, power washers, leaf blowers, and anything else you can get your hands on.

LIGHT BULBS

Screwing a light bulb in or out of the light fixture creates a good metal squeak. If you have permission, drop the light bulb and record the crash. For a fun session, build up a collection of burned out light bulbs and smash them all at once!

MONSTER GROWLS

You can release the beast within by giving your best monster growl into the microphone and pitching the sound down for a terrifying roar. A good technique when recording monster voices is to record your voice into a garbage can, bucket, or other objects to give your voice deeper resonance. There are great plug-ins out there like Digital Brain Instrument's Voxpat Player that can instantly transform any voice into a horrifying creature!

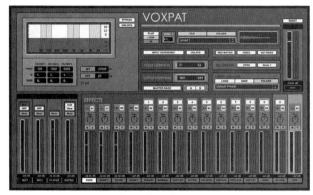

Voxpat Vocal Plug-In

MUD

You can record really cool mud suction sounds by mixing dirt in a bucket and using a plunger. Start with a little amount of water and record the different dirt/water ratios as you add more water. Careful! The more water you add the messier it will get. You can pour the bucket out for vomit sounds. Thick mud bubbles can be pitch-shifted and layered to create the sound of flowing lava.

Using a Toilet Plunger to create Mud Suction Sounds

MUSICAL INSTRUMENTS

Record the musical instruments that your family has and remember that they make more than just musical sounds. Percussion instruments provided many of the traditional cartoon sound effects. Watch old cartoons like Looney Tunes for some inspiration for things to record.

NEIGHBORHOOD AMBIENCE

The sound of your neighborhood will change throughout the day. For example, birds and insects tend to be more vocal in the morning and evening hours, kids are more active in the middle of the day, traffic is more frequent around rush hour times, etc. Plan your sessions around these times, or even better, record each time frame. Changes in the season will also change the sound of your neighborhood, depending on where you live. For example, insects are more vocal during warmer seasons, birds fly south during the winter, etc.

OFFICE SUPPLIES

Everyone has a junk drawer with random office supplies like staplers, scissors, hole punches, and a billion different writing utensils. Spend an afternoon going through the drawer recording these items, and don't forget to record the sound of the items going in and out of the drawer.

PAPER

Ripping paper can be a cool sound to use with other sounds to create new sound effects. For example, I used the sound of paper ripping as the sound of a mortar shell falling from the sky that was used in the Call Of Duty video game series. Experiment with what you've recorded and try to use them in new and unconventional ways. There are tons of sound to explore!

PETS

You've spent a lot of effort trying to quiet your pets while you record, now it's time to let them make some noise! The catch is, animals only perform when they want to, so it might take some coaxing to get your pet to cooperate. Have some treats ready to help motivate and reward your pet. Remember to be kind to your pet. Never stress or hurt an animal to get them to perform.

PHONES

A smartphone comes preloaded with ringtones that can be recorded by placing the microphone near the speaker of the smartphone. You don't need to have someone call you. Simply preview the ringtone sound from the settings menu. You can loop the sound later as many times as you would like. Keep in mind; ringtones are copyrighted material, so you won't be able to sell those recordings.

If you make your own ringtones, you can make them sound like they are coming from a cell phone by using an equalizer and keeping only the frequencies between 300Hz–5kHz. Of course, you can always play your own ringtones through your smartphone and record them using a technique known as "worldizing." Worldizing is the process of rerecording a sound by playing the sound through a speaker in a specific environment or space. The technique was developed by sound legend Randy Thom of Skywalker Sound.

PIRATE CHEST

Use a footlocker or wooden trunk for the sound of a pirate's chest. The chest will sound hollow if it's empty, so don't forget to add some weight (unless the pirates are about to discover that there's no treasure...). Use large or pitch-shifted coins for gold bullions. If you don't have enough coins for your booty, record additional tracks of coins and layer them together.

Recording Swords while pretending to be a Pirate

PLAYING CARDS

Record a deck of cards shuffling, cutting, dealing, etc. You can even add the sound of chips betting for a poker game.

PNEUMATIC BURSTS

Bottles of carbonated soda are great sources for science fiction pneumatic bursts. Shake the bottle gently to build up pressure before opening the cap. Give the cap a quick turn without removing the cap. This will allow you to record the sound of the pressure release without hearing the cap. Be careful not to shake the bottle too much, because although it's fun to watch soda spill everywhere, it really doesn't make much sound. Also, make sure that the microphone is protected from any spray from the soda.

POWER TOOLS

Record the activities of home improvement projects. You can set up the recorder while you work on a home project and get the ambience of a job site. With permission and supervision, you can also record the individual tools like drills, saws, and air compressors. When working with power tools, be sure to have building materials handy for the tools to interact with.

PUNCHES

Slapstick comedies got their name from a sound effect prop that consisted of two small wood planks that would be slapped together to create punch and slap sounds. This prop was frequently used in the early years of Hollywood, but its origins date back to the sixteenth century!

Some of the most iconic punch sound effects came from the Indiana Jones movie series. For the punches in those films, legendary sound designer Ben Burtt used a baseball bat and hit leather jackets stuffed with baseball gloves. You can use any sound that has a tough, fleshy sound. Layering multiple sounds together and letting the sound distort a little can create harder punches and lowering the pitch will make the punch sound heavier.

And no, punches don't sound like that in real life; so don't try to convince your friends to let you record hitting them.

The Wrong Way to Record a Punch with Professional MMA Trainer Brandon Gallo

RADIO STATIC

The white noise of radio static is a very useful sound to have. Pitching the sound down a little bit can create a waterfall sound. Pitching the sound down a lot can create an earthquake rumble. If you don't have a radio in your home, you can record a radio inside a car or use a noise generator.

RAIN AMBIENCE

The obvious challenge with recording rain is keeping the gear dry. One of the tricks that I've used over the years is placing the recorder inside the garage with the door open during a rainstorm. This allows the recorder to hear the rain without getting wet. Be careful how close to the door you place the recorder. Rainstorms are often accompanied by strong gusts of wind, which can blow rain into the garage and all over your gear.

You can use a garden hose to simulate rain, especially if you'd like to record rain on different surfaces like grass, cars, aluminum awnings, or other surfaces that might not be close enough to your garage door to record during a rainstorm. The hose will allow you to create rain anytime you'd like! For larger rainstorms, layer several recordings together.

Poking holes in the lid of a milk jug can be used for constant rain/water drips. You can refill the milk jug as many times as you like and edit the sounds together for one continuous rainstorm.

ROLLER SKATES

To record roller skates in motion, you're going to need to follow the action. This means that you will need to move alongside the person who is roller-skating. You don't want to hear the sound of your footsteps in the recording, so you may need to take off your shoes. Another trick is for you to wear the roller skates and record yourself skating. Be aware of potential wind noise while in motion.

SHEET WARBLES

Garage sale signs and other large plastic sheets can create funny cartoon warbles when you move them back and forth. Large metal sheets and signs can also sound like rolling thunder.

SHOWERS

Most showers have a natural reverb in the sound that can be useful for ambient water drips in a cave or sewer. Vary the flow of water from the showerhead from flowing full force to intermittent drips of water. You can record the shower up close or you can place the recorder outside of the shower or even outside of the room for a more distant sound.

SKATEBOARDS

Skateboards in motion are recorded using the same technique as roller skates. You don't need to be Tony Hawk to record great skateboard tricks. Simply use your hands to perform the tricks with the skateboard. Remember, they can't *see* what you are doing but they can *hear* what you are doing, so make it sound cool!

SNOW

If you can't wait until winter to record snow or if you live in a warmer climate, you can simulate snow by using cornstarch. This technique has been a Hollywood tradition for footsteps in snow for nearly a century. Plus, you don't have to worry about bundling up for the cold. If you live in an area that gets snow in the winter, be sure to record as much snow elements as you can before it melts. Don't forget to record sleds, snowballs, body falls and other actions in the snow.

SPACESHIP INTERIOR

If you are looking for the perfect ambience to use in the hallway of the alien's mother ship, you can record your furnace or even a bathroom fan and pitch the sound down several octaves. It can be helpful to pitch-layer the recording, adding air hoses and beeps to complete the effect. You can also experiment with synthesizers or combine your recording with electronic sounds. Remember, the spaceship isn't of this world, so nobody knows what it's suppose to sound like. Make us believe!

SPORTING GOODS

Find as many athletic supplies as you can and spend an afternoon recording all the fun. You can record things like baseball bats, gloves, basketballs, footballs, soccer balls, tennis balls, dodgeballs, and volleyballs.

STAIRS

Footsteps on stairs can be simulated, but nothing beats the sound of the real thing. Follow the action with the microphone or stand at the top or bottom of the stairs and let the footsteps come to you. You can also place the microphone above and below the stairs for different perspectives.

STINGERS

Stingers are the slams and hits that you hear during movie trailers when the titles appear on the screen or during a cut or transition. These sounds are often a blend of explosions and metal impacts layered together. Stingers often have a suction effect that happens before the impact. You can easily create this effect by copying the impact, reversing that copy, and then layering it on top of the original sound. You can make the impact pop even more by placing the reversed sound first and leaving a brief space between the reversed sound and the impact. Fading out the reversed sound before the impact can also make the impact hit harder. With some moderate sound design skills and the right sound sources, you can create a cool soundtrack for your next epic trailer.

STONE DOOR

You can create realistic stone doors for crypts, ancient tombs or forbidden temples by using a large plastic storage bin. Place the bin upside down on concrete and slowly slide the bin in front of the microphone. The empty cavity inside the bin will give the sound a deeper resonance. The larger the bin, the bigger the door will sound. For a grittier sound, place some rock salt on the concrete first.

Recording a Stone Door with a Plastic Bin

SWIMMING POOL

If you or a willing neighbor has a pool, you can record swimming, splashes, dives, cannonballs, and all sorts of wet sounds. The trick is to get close enough to the action without getting wet. Of course, if you have a hydrophone, you can record more action below the surface.

SWING SET

A swing set or jungle gym can be a great resource for metal squeaks and wood creaks. You may need a friend to help add weight to the swings. The added weight can deepen the pitch of the squeaks and creaks.

TEAKETTLE

The high pitch whistle from a teakettle is worth the wait, even though it might seem like it takes forever. Try raising and lowering the pitch to see what cool sounds you can make.

TOILETS

Toilet flushes can be recorded up close and personal or from a distance for perspective. The water refilling the toilet can take a long time, so you might want to shorten or edit the refill sound all together leaving you with a classic flush sound. Also, the next time the toilet gets plugged up, don't forget to record the plunger and gurgle sounds.

TOOLS

A toolbox can be a treasure chest of sound effects. Here are some sounds that you can make with tools:

- Ratchets can be used for gears or even giant drawbridge chains if you pitch the sound down low enough.
- Vice grips make good metal clicking sounds.
- Hammers are great for banging against anything you want to make noise with. Personally, I prefer sledgehammers…
- Saw blades can make great warbling sounds when shaken back and forth. Be careful of the saw's teeth. They will bite you!
- Staple guns are perfect for recording a pistol drop.

And since you're digging through the toolbox, be sure to record it too. You can record the toolbox being picked up, set down, sliding, opening and closing.

TOYS

A Slinky is a great source for cool sounds. If you extend the Slinky with one hand so that the spring is stretched with the bottom on the ground, you can hit the Slinky to create a laser blast sound. If you have never owned a Slinky, put this book down and race to the store before your childhood is officially ruined!

TRAINS

Trains are loud. You will need to keep a distance from the train tracks so that your sounds won't be distorted as well as for obvious safety reasons. If you are near an intersection you can also record the crossing bell. The crossing bell will ring prior to the train approaching. If possible, record a clean take of the bell before and after the train has passed. You can edit out the train passing and keep just the crossing bell by looping and splicing the track. It cannot be stressed enough how dangerous trains are! Always keep a safe distance and never go closer to a train than the sidewalk.

TRASH CANS

If you have to take out the trash, you might as well record it. Record the sounds of garbage bags going into trash cans as well as trash being thrown into garbage cans. Metal trashcan lids can be spun and rolled to create the sound of a runaway hubcap. You can also slam the lid for a gunshot.

UMBRELLAS

The sound of an umbrella opening and closing can be used for all sorts of fun stuff like photo flash bulbs, creature wings, and superhero capes. When recording an umbrella, keep in mind that there is a fair amount of air that is pushed away from the umbrella when it is moved quickly. You will need to experiment with the placement of the microphone to make sure that the sound is recorded without the air movement.

UNDERWATER SOUNDS

Hydrophones are special waterproof microphones specifically designed to record underwater. Some of the professional hydrophones can be pretty expensive, but you can find some for under $100 on the internet. If you don't want to buy a special microphone just for underwater sounds, you can always process regular water sounds by pitching the recordings down and experimenting with EQ.

WALKIE-TALKIES

To record a conversation on walkie-talkies, place a microphone next to one walkie-talkie and use the other walkie-talkie in a different room. This will allow the sound of the voice to be heard through only the walkie-talkie. Some walkie-talkies include a button that sends a beep that can be used for Morse code. You don't need to record every letter in the alphabet. Instead, record a couple of long and short beeps and edit the sounds together to create letters, words or phrases that you'd like. Also, don't forget to record static, tuning, turning the walkie-talkies on/off and whatever else you can think of.

Here is the Morse code:

Letter	Morse		
A	.−	T	−
B	−...	U	..−
C	−.−.	V	...−
D	−..	W	.− −
E	.	X	−..−
F	..−.	Y	−.− −
G	− −.	Z	− −..
H	....	0	− − − − −
I	..	1	.− − − −
J	.− − −	2	..− − −
K	−.−	3	...− −
L	.−..	4	....−
M	− −	5	.....
N	−.	6	−....
O	− − −	7	− −...
P	.−.	8	− − −..
Q	− −.−	9	− − − −.
R	.−.		
S	...		

Note that a "." represents a short beep and a "−" represents a long beep.

VOMIT

If you need to create the sound of someone barfing, you don't need to wait until they're sick. Simply use a can of soup (or large pot of soup depending on how sick you want the person to sound) to simulate someone throwing up their lunch into the toilet. And don't forget to record the sound of the flush! For the sound of the vomit splashing on pavement, you can use the garage floor. You can also add the sound of someone heaving for a grosser effect.

WALLA TRACKS

In the movie business, a walla track is the name given for the background sound of people talking. Usually, the words are indistinguishable and are meant to serve as a drone of voices. If you don't have a big group of people, you can always layer and pitch the voices of a small group to make the group sound bigger.

Here are some things to record with your group, including some Foley movements:

- Applause
- Booing
- Crying
- Disagreeing
- Giggling
- Laughing
- Mumbling
- Screaming
- Sighing

- Talking
- Whispering

WATERFALLS

Radio or television static can be pitched to create a convincing waterfall. The lower the pitch, the larger the waterfall will sound. If you have a fountain in your backyard you can record, the takes can be edited together to also create a waterfall or be added to the static recordings.

WHIPS

Dowel rods are perfect for making whooshing sounds like a fast cut in a television show or an object being thrown. Whips are great sounds to add to punches to give the sound of the fist moving through the air. To record these types of sounds, place the microphone perpendicular to the dowel rod. The larger the rod the heavier the sound, and the thinner the rod the higher in pitch the sound. Be sure to use wind protection because the rod will push air into the microphone, which could spoil the take.

For arrow twangs, place the rod on a flat surface with a few inches hanging off the side and pluck the end of the rod. The shorter the end of the rod hanging off the surface is, the higher the pitch of the twang will be. The longer the end is, the lower the pitch of the twang will be.

You can make the sound of an object spiraling by layering and cutting multiple whip sounds together. Try making a thirty-second sound effect of whips cut together. Then, pitch it way up and see what it sounds like.

You can also use cords and twirl them overhead like a lasso to create constant whipping sounds. If there is no room overhead, you can twirl the cords vertically. Be sure to position the microphone to eliminate air movement and protection from any accidents. Using a cord can create a convincing bullwhip sound once you add a crack sound at the end from a firecracker, handclap or rubber glove snap.

WIND

A windy day is a great opportunity to record wind, but there are ways to record wind without nature's help. With a little bit of design work, you can turn vocalized wind sounds into a giant blizzard with some pitching and layering. Placing the microphone near a screen door or slightly cracked window can provide very useful recordings on days when nature is cooperating.

WRITING UTENSILS

Use various surfaces to write on like paper or cardboard and record pencils, ink pens and markers. For realistic performances, pay attention to what you are writing by spelling real words and sentences. Record performing the actions at different speeds and lengths. For example, the sound of an ink pen filling out a form sounds different than an ink pen signing a contract. Remember, performance is important!

ZIPPERS

Zippers come in all shapes and sizes. Pants zippers sound different than zippers on a duffle bag. Zippers are everywhere. From school backpacks to winter coats, you can find zippers in every closet in the house. Record as many zippers as you can find.

ZOMBIES

Fortunately, you won't have to board up the house and take shelter to record these sounds. Just like with monster sounds, you can record zombie sounds with your voice. It can be helpful to have a glass of water handy for gargling and wetter growls. For a group of zombies, record a bunch of your friends or siblings. You can lower the pitch of the recordings to make the voices sound older.

If the zombies are hungry for some flesh, grab some watermelon and cantaloupes to make the juicy gore sounds. Celery twists can be added for bone snaps during the chomps. You can let your hands do all the work or you can eat the fruit while snarling for a more realistic sound. Not that I'm suggesting that zombies are real...

This is just the tip of the iceberg! Every house is different. Be sure to explore your house and ask your parents, family members and neighbors for unique things that you can record. Use your imagination and always be listening for cool sounds to record.

**The Poster for the Zombie Apocalypse Sound Effects Library
painted by Detroit artist Matt Busch**

— SEAN'S NOTES —

Use these different ways to create a sound as ideas and branch off of them to form your own sounds. In the past, I have recorded numerous sounds. I have done vocals for short films, I have recorded things around my house, and I've gotten to smash many things in the Foley Room. Just remember to be creative and have fun recording and editing your sound effects.

CHAPTER 10

MAKE SOME NOISE!

In this book we have discussed the process of making sound effects, including the tools, techniques, and even sources around the house to create your own sound effects. But this book would not be complete without discussing the one essential ingredient: creativity. I cannot stress enough the importance of creativity. While this book has given you some ideas and even the Ten Recording Commandments, remember that some rules are meant to be broken—or at least bent to the point of breaking. Always trust your gut instincts. Just because someone hasn't tried something before doesn't mean you shouldn't. Play. Experiment. Make mistakes!

When I first started creating sound effects I knew nothing about the process. I borrowed some recording gear and went out into the woods one day just for fun. I loved it so much that it led to a very successful career and I became the world's largest independent producer of sound effects for the motion picture, television, and video game industries. While I would've loved to have a book like this when I first started, all I had to rely on in the beginning was my creativity. I made a lot of mistakes, but mistakes aren't a bad thing. When you learn from a mistake it instantly becomes a lesson—and lessons are a good thing!

To this day, I still try things I normally wouldn't do just to see what they sound like. I still play with objects to hear what sounds they can make and try different miking techniques. The sound effects industry is only a century old, so there is a lot of unexplored territory out there. When in doubt about a sound, record it anyways. You don't have to use the sound, but at least you'll know what it sounds like. You'll never know until you try . . .

I am very grateful to industry professionals like Alan Howarth, Rob Nokes, Charles Maynes, Steve Lee, Charlie Campagna, Dan Kerr, Scott Gershin, Frank Bry, Watson Wu, Aaron Marks, Marc Fishman, David Sonnenschein, David Farmer, Stephan Schutze, Michael Orlowski, Dave Chmela, Colin Hart, Vanessa Theme Ament, and countless others who have helped me on my journey in the world of sound effects. Their advice and friendship have helped me become the sound effects creator that I am today. I encourage you to research their work to help you develop your own skills, and once you have, be sure to help others too!

You can find tons of cool tips and tricks from Facebook groups, message boards, and forums. The internet is full of useful information from Academy Award-winning sound designers, industry professionals, freelancers, and beginners just like you. Who knows? Maybe one day you'll become a leading pioneer in the sound effects industry! The only person that can decide that is you, so press record and make some noise!

— SEAN'S NOTES —

Creativity is the core of creating sound effects. Sometimes I find it can be difficult to be creative in some situations, so I like to use inspiration to drive my creativity. Personally, I love to watch movies for inspiration and certain genres can inspire you to create certain sound effects. For example, watching movies like Star Wars can inspire you to create science fiction sound effects, or watching movies like Die Hard or Lethal Weapon can inspire you to create action sound effects. Remember that the sky is the limit and to be creative. Happy recording!

# ABOUT THE
AUTHORS

Ric Viers is a sound designer and author based in Detroit, Michigan. Ric is the world's largest producer of professional sound effects libraries with more than 670 products produced to date. He is the owner of SoundEffects.com, author of *The Sound Effects Bible* and *The Location Sound Bible*, and the founder of Blastwave FX—one of the world's leading sound effects publishers. His location sound credits include hundreds of productions for nearly every major television network, Universal Studios, Dateline, Good Morning America, Disney, and many others. Known as the "Rock and Roll Professor of Sound," Viers was inducted into the Full Sail University Hall of Fame in 2014 and has hosted several video series like *Rode University, Rode Rage,* and most notably *The Detroit Chop Shop Video Diaries*—a YouTube-based reality series about the interns at his studio, The Detroit Chop Shop. His sound design work continues to be used in major motion pictures, television shows, radio programs, and video games worldwide. For more information visit http://www.ricviers.com.

Sean Viers is a sound effects enthusiast, filmmaker, and Lego lover. He has a third degree black belt in karate and a first degree black belt in Modern Arnis. Sean was a member of the National Junior Honors Society, president of the student council, and plays the drums, bass guitar, and saxophone. He doesn't like to brag, so his dad had to write his bio for him.

Sean Viers and Ric Viers having a Diet Coke and smile...

FULL SAIL
U N I V E R S I T Y®

Top 25 Global Music Programs
– Hollywood Reporter (2015)

Bring your
Sound to Life

**Campus & Online
Degrees Available**

Audio Production

Music Business

Music Production

Recording Arts

Show Production

800.226.7625   fullsail.edu

THE SOUND
OF SILENCE

The RØDE NT-1 is the quietest microphone in the world.
With an imperceptible 4.5dBA self-noise, the RØDE NT-1
is the blank canvas upon which you can create
your masterpiece.

Make some noise.

RØDE NT1
1″ Condenser
Microphone
Made in Australia

www.rode.com

THE SOUND EFFECTS BIBLE
HOW TO CREATE AND RECORD HOLLYWOOD STYLE SOUND EFFECTS

RIC VIERS

The Sound Effects Bible is a complete guide to recording and editing sound effects. The book covers topics such as microphone selection, field recorders, the ABCs of digital audio, understanding Digital Audio Workstations, building your own Foley stage, designing your own editing studio, and more.

"Ric's book is an excellent introduction to techniques for producing professional sound effects for films, games, etc. It's packed with nuts-and-bolts information that beginning and intermediate level sound designers/editors will find useful."

— Randy Thom, director of sound design, Skywalker Sound

"Ric Viers eats, drinks, and breathes sound effects. If you're a sound designer, editor, or filmmaker, you'll need the Bible!"

— Tasos Frantzolas, founder of Soundsnap.com

"The Sound Effects Bible is the go-to resource for anyone serious about sound creation! Ric Viers generously shares his real-world experience in an absorbing and hard to put down guide to this fascinating corner of the entertainment industry."

— Aaron Marks, composer/sound designer and author of The Complete Guide to Game Audio

RIC VIERS is a sound designer and author based in Detroit, Michigan. Ric is the world's largest producer of professional sound effects libraries with more than 670 products produced to date. He is the owner of SoundEffects.com, author of The Sound Effects Bible and The Location Sound Bible, and the founder of Blastwave FX—one of the world's leading sound effects publishers. His location sound credits include hundreds of productions for nearly every major television network, Universal Studios, Dateline, Good Morning America, Disney, and many others. Known as the "Rock and Roll Professor of Sound," Viers was inducted into the Full Sail University Hall of Fame in 2014 and has hosted several video series like Rode University, Rode Rage, and most notably The Detroit Chop Shop Video Diaries—a YouTube-based reality series about the interns at his studio, The Detroit Chop Shop. His sound design work continues to be used in major motion pictures, television shows, radio programs, and video games worldwide. For more information visit http://www.ricviers.com.

$26.95 · 260 PAGES · ORDER #90RLS · ISBN 9781932907483

THE LOCATION SOUND BIBLE
HOW TO CREATE AND RECORD HOLLYWOOD STYLE
SOUND EFFECTS

RIC VIERS

The Location Sound Bible explains how to achieve Hollywood-quality sound that will make your productions stand out from the rest. From audio basics and microphone selection to the business side of show biz, this book takes you behind the scenes of Viers' work on feature films, television shows, broadcast news, courtroom dramas, and music videos.

"The Location Sound Bible *is the first truly comprehensive guide to the acquisition of on-set production sound. I will recommend it to all of my students."*
> — Peter Damski C.A.S., Production Sound Mixer, *Mad About You,*
> *Will & Grace, Hannah Montana*

"Ric Viers takes an in-depth look into the world of location recording. A must-read for those wanting to learn about dialog and FX recording or recording in general. He covers the theory, the techniques, and the technology. Once you finish this book, you'll start listening to the world around you a whole lot differently."
> — Scott Martin Gershin, Sound Designer/Sound Supervisor/Mixer,
> *Braveheart, Gladiator, Star Trek*

"Ric Viers unveils the mysteries of location recording for film and Electronic News Gathering, using technical detail seasoned with humor. As a post-production professional and dialog editor, I know how critical it is to get beautiful sound when the camera rolls. "
> — David Stone, IATSE, Supervising Sound Editor; Academy Award
> recipient, Best Sound Effects Editing, *Bram Stoker's Dracula*

RIC VIERS is a sound designer and author based in Detroit, Michigan. Ric is the world's largest producer of professional sound effects libraries with more than 670 products produced to date. He is the owner of SoundEffects.com, author of *The Sound Effects Bible* and *The Location Sound Bible*, and the founder of Blastwave FX—one of the world's leading sound effects publishers. His location sound credits include hundreds of productions for nearly every major television network, Universal Studios, Dateline, Good Morning America, Disney, and many others.

$26.95 · 376 PAGES · ORDER #185RLS · ISBN 9781615931200

FILMMAKING FOR TEENS – 2ND EDITION
PULLING OFF YOUR SHORTS

TROY LANIER AND CLAY NICHOLS

With over 20 hours of video being uploaded to YouTube every minute, how can a young filmmaker possibly stand out? By reading and applying the tools of *Filmmaking for Teens* young filmmakers can learn everything they need to know about how to make a great short film.

The updated edition of this classic manual includes numerous additions reflecting the enormous changes impacting the world of digital video.

"Redesigned to be even easier to understand and packed with more up-to-date information on digital filmmaking, the 2nd edition of Filmmaking for Teens *should be the essential textbook for schools and community centers that want to provide a high-quality filmmaking curriculum for their students.""*
> — Toby M. Bronson, Set Costumer, *Pirates of the Caribbean*, *The Aviator*, *Deadwood*

*"*Filmmaking for Teens *is an exceptional filmmaking guide for anyone determined to create their own film. Written by Troy Lanier and Clay Nichols,* Filmmaking for Teens *is a simple, easy to understand guide to improving amateur videos."*
> — Amanda Porter, Associate Editor, *School Video News*

*"*Filmmaking for Teens *is a 7-11 full of every filmmaking goodie you'll need to write, shoot, edit and show a short film that people will actually want to see, using the resources you already have: friends, parents, no money, and a long weekend. From how to finish a script, to when to go handheld, to how to mooch equipment, to what won't work, this book is all you need to get your filmmaking career started."*
> — Alex Epstein, Author, *Crafty Screenwriting* and *Crafty TV Writing*, co-writer of the hit comedy film *Bon Cop Bad Cop*

Since publishing the first edition, TROY LANIER and CLAY NICHOLS have gone on to become pioneers in the online video industry. Producers of the acclaimed series *DadLabs*, the pair has produced over 500 episodes of WebTV that have garnered millions of viewers. These masters of online video have put into practice the principles of this book.

$20.95 · 224 PAGES · ORDER #137RLS · ISBN 9781932907681

SHOOTING BETTER MOVIES
THE STUDENT FILMMAKERS' GUIDE

PAUL DUDBRIDGE

A one-stop film school, this book is packed with information, tips, techniques, and advice covering all aspects of filmmaking as gathered from the author's years of experience working in short films, features, commercials, and music videos, as well as delivering workshops and lectures to film students of all ages. Everything you need to know – from generating an idea to delivering a finished film – is laid out in an informal and easy-to-read style.

Shooting Movies
THE STUDENT FILMMAKERS' GUIDE

Paul Dudbridge

"Nailed it! A simple, turbo-fast read. A practical, no-nonsense, encouraging guide to filmmaking. Students of film, from the initiate to the updating pro, will enrich their knowledge and confidence with Shooting Better Movies. Where was this when I started?"
> – Pen Densham, Oscar-nominated writer, producer, director, Trilogy Entertainment Group principal, *Robin Hood: Prince of Thieves, Backdraft, Moll Flanders, Blown Away, Tank Girl, Outer Limits*

"A valuable resource for anyone starting out on their filmmaking journey."
> – Dr. Neil Fox, Course Coordinator, BA (Hons) Film, Falmouth University, UK

"Dudbridge orchestrates within this do-it-yourself manual a stirring and sustained call to action: while providing a well-structured, informative guide to the essential principles and practice of filmmaking, he never stops emphasizing the importance of learning through the experiences of real-world film production. His passion and persuasiveness are equally infectious. If you are serious about making your student films stand out from their competition, you need to read this book."
> – Stephen Gordon, Senior Lecturer in Film Production Technology, Birmingham City University (UK)

PAUL DUDBRIDGE is a British director, producer, cinematographer, and educator, making feature films, television, commercials, and music videos. His work as a cinematographer includes the action thriller *By Any Name*, based on the bestselling book by Katherine John.

$26.95 · 186 PAGES · ORDER #247RLS · ISBN 9781615932719

WRITE! SHOOT! EDIT!
A COMPLETE GUIDE FOR TEEN FILMMAKERS

DEBORAH S. PATZ

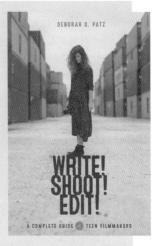

You're a teenager who loves movies but has no way to learn filmmaking ... until now! This book lets your spread your creative-storytelling wings through three interconnected skill sets — writing, shooting, and editing.

You want to direct and edit, but your friend wants to write? Not a problem. Don't read the book in order! Just follow the path. *Write! Shoot! Edit!* is written in three distinct and inter-twining paths, so you can experience the book as you want to: as a writer, director / DOP, or editor.

"A thorough, dynamic, and inspiring guide for young filmmakers written in the voice of a mentor who challenges but never underestimates her audience. It could be life-changing in the hands of a motivated teenager working on their own, and it's ideal as a text for high school media courses."
> —Bruce Sheridan, professor and chair, Cinema Art and Science, Columbia College Chicago

"An engaging book for teens, and a wealth of information about movie making for all ages, now on our school must-read list for students and staff."
> —Trevor Kolkea, principal, École Moody Middle School of the Arts

"A helpful and detailed yet easy-to-read and understand guide for aspiring filmmakers—with a focus on teens. Using language younger creative minds can understand and engage with, Patz is ensuring the next generation of emerging screen-based artists is armed with the keys to success in the industry."
> —Kim Hsu Guise, director of content, Local and Original Programming, TELUS

DEBORAH S. PATZ has been a professional in the film industry since the mid-1980s, with a filmography that spans family and children's programming, science-fiction extravaganzas, and feature films of various budget sizes.

$23.95 · 160 PAGES · ORDER #246RLS · ISBN 9781615932641

THE MYTH OF MWP

In a dark time, a light bringer came along, leading the curious and the frustrated to clarity and empowerment. It took the well-guarded secrets out of the hands of the few and made them available to all. It spread a spirit of openness and creative freedom, and built a storehouse of knowledge dedicated to the betterment of the arts.

The essence of the Michael Wiese Productions (MWP) is empowering people who have the burning desire to express themselves creatively. We help them realize their dreams by putting the tools in their hands. We demystify the sometimes secretive worlds of screenwriting, directing, acting, producing, film financing, and other media crafts.

By doing so, we hope to bring forth a realization of 'conscious media' which we define as being positively charged, emphasizing hope and affirming positive values like trust, cooperation, self-empowerment, freedom, and love. Grounded in the deep roots of myth, it aims to be healing both for those who make the art and those who encounter it. It hopes to be transformative for people, opening doors to new possibilities and pulling back veils to reveal hidden worlds.

MWP has built a storehouse of knowledge unequaled in the world, for no other publisher has so many titles on the media arts. Please visit www.mwp.com where you will find many free resources and a 25% discount on our books. Sign up and become part of the wider creative community!

Onward and upward,

Michael Wiese
Publisher/Filmmaker